Praise for
***Taking the Scenic Route to Manhood*:**

"I was fascinated with *Taking the Scenic Route to Manhood*. Finally a book that sheds light on what a spirit can go through when it receives a body that doesn't match what it desires to be. It is highly humorous, yet compelling and well thought out. What I loved about this book is how grounded and informative Jeremy makes this serious subject."

— David Armstrong, Author of *Messages from the Spirit World*

"*Taking the Scenic Route to Manhood* will change your way of thinking in such a profound way! We all have a heart and our heart has a strong desire to find its calling. As humans, we are so fragile in the face of judgment, but when we learn to clear our minds and let our hearts lead, we will find the strength to conquer ourselves and stand within our truth. This book is a powerful reminder of the power of self!"

— Nicole Gabriel, Author of *Finding Your Inner Truth*

"Every now and then, I run across a book that truly shares the warmth and goodness of the human spirit. This book is one of those masterpieces. Jeremy Wallace has done a fantastic job exposing his struggles to the world, allowing us to get inside his mind, as he transforms himself into a newer, more passionate individual destined to achieve his goals. This book is truly a 'caterpillar to a butterfly' story that you can embrace and enjoy, and feel forever changed after reading it. Kudos, a brilliant piece of work!"

— Patrick Snow, International Best-Selling Author of *Creating Your Own Destiny*, *The Affluent Entrepreneur*, and *Boy Entrepreneur*

"No matter our sexual orientation, gender, color, or religion, we all have secret desires to live our lives to the fullest. Most of us fear showing our true selves to others. But Jeremy Wallace embraced his desires, controlled his fear, and did what his heart told him to do—to become the man he knew he should be. Read this book, laugh, cry, be inspired, and then follow his example of being true to yourself."

— Tyler R. Tichelaar, Ph.D., and Award-Winning Author of *The Best Place* and *Arthur's Legacy*

"Written with enormous sensitivity, this powerful book is of value to family, friends, clergy, teachers, helping professionals, and anyone who cares about the challenges faced by those who seek to change their physical appearance to match their gender identity."

— Susan Friedmann, CSP, International Best-Selling Author of *Riches in Niches: How to Make it BIG in a Small Market*

"*Taking the Scenic Route to Manhood* is a soulfully written account of a very real and trying experience. How one person can go through so much and grow so gracefully through it all makes this a must read for anyone struggling to be accepted in this world."

— James F. Johnson, Author of *Bullies & Allies*

TAKING THE SCENIC ROUTE TO MANHOOD

A JOURNEY OF CHANGE AND TRANSFORMATION

JEREMY L. WALLACE

Taking the Scenic Route to Manhood
A Journey of Change and Transformation
Copyright 2015 by Jeremy L. Wallace

Published by:
Aviva Publishing
Lake Placid, NY
(518) 523-1320
www.AvivaPubs.com

All rights reserved. No part of this publication may be reproduced, stored in a retrieval system, or transmitted in any form or by any means, electronic, mechanical, photocopying, recording, scanning, or otherwise, without the prior written permission of the author. Address all inquiries to:

Jeremy L. Wallace
Telephone: 303-810-4071

Email: Jeremy@JeremyLWallace.com
www.JeremyLWallace.com
www.TakingThe ScenicRouteToManhood.com

ISBN: 978-1-940984-68-1

Library of Congress # 2014918003

Editor: Tyler Tichelaar
Jacket Design: Nicole Gabriel / Angel Dog Productions
Interior Book Design: Nicole Gabriel / Angel Dog Productions
Author Photo: Fred Morledge – PhotoFM.com

Every attempt has been made to source properly all quotes.

Printed in the United States of America

First Edition

10 9 8 7 6 5 4 3 2 1

For additional copies visit:
www.JeremyLWallace.com

DEDICATION

To my parents, Jerry and Jacky, for not only bringing me into this world, but for loving and supporting me the entire journey. Both of you have taught me so many life lessons that have shaped me into the man I am today, and your tireless patience, guidance, and unwavering love have made everything in my life possible. You created a foundation of safety and security in my life and always encouraged me to be myself. I am blessed beyond measure to have you as my parents, and I am the luckiest kid in the world.

To my sister, Jayna, who has been my true partner in life, mentor, and guardian angel. From the very beginning, you have been right by my side, building me up when I didn't believe in myself and have put the pieces back together when life was falling apart. Your selfless compassion and support has allowed me to take the leap of faith to become my true self. I thank you from the bottom of my heart and know that this journey wouldn't have been possible without you.

To my kids (dogs), Dolly and Madison, for their unconditional love, especially when change and uncertainty were everywhere. They have always known when to kiss away my tears of pain and how to brighten my days. Their gentle nudges saved me when my world seemed too big to go on. They are, undeniably, little gifts from God.

To Jesus Christ, without Him in my life, I would not be alive today. Through His grace, He has given me the strength and courage to live authentically and honestly. He has and always will be with me every step of the way, guiding my path.

To Jenny, who was strong enough to come into this world and survive thirty-eight years of turmoil. It was her resilience and courage that built the foundation for the man that was to come. She reached out her hand and helped to usher in Jeremy, and in the midst of transition, it took the strength of two people, until the day that she knew Jeremy was strong enough to stand tall on his own. It was then that I reached out my hand and escorted her out with love and gratitude.

ACKNOWLEDGMENTS

I would like to thank the following people for their support of my journey and bringing this book to fruition:

Jennifer Andrews, Dr. Michael Brownstein, Dr. Curtis Crane, Sandi Daileda, Kristin Edholm, Susan Friedmann, Nicole Gabriel, Rayshelle Gamponia, Jane Heenan, Juniper Lusk, Patrick Loya, Jay McConnell, Jayna McConnell, Sidney McConnell, Sara Mildebrandt, Fred Morledge, Belinda Ruelle, Gerald Rhodes, Kris Smith, Patrick Snow, Janice Stevens, Tyler Tichelaar, Dr. David Tusek, Jacky Wallace, Jerry Wallace, Judy Wallace, and Cheryl Wells.

CONTENTS

Foreword by David Tusek, M.D.   11

Chapter 1:   It's a Boy…er, Girl?   15
Chapter 2:   Change Is Brewing   27
Chapter 3:   Finding the Courage to Jump   53
Chapter 4:   Let's Get This Party Started   75
Chapter 5:   Look Out, a Hurricane Is Coming   101
Chapter 6:   Puberty 2.0   113
Chapter 7:   Behind Every Great Man Is a Great Woman   129
Chapter 8:   To Pee or Not To Pee   143
Chapter 9:   Paperwork and Red Tape   157
Chapter 10:   Fearing Fear   173
Chapter 11:   Putting the Pieces Together   189
Chapter 12:   What's Missing?   205
Chapter 13:   Coming Full Circle   223
Chapter 14:   The Six Million Dollar Transman   241

A Final Note: You Are Not Alone   259

Resources   269
About the Author   275
Book Jeremy L. Wallace to Speak at Your Next Event   277

FOREWORD

It is an act of grace and courage to love the world enough to honor one's life with the dignity of authenticity. Who among us is unfamiliar with the fear of resistance from external forces that seems to exist only to oppose our very self-actualization and the manifestation of our undeniable dreams? But overcoming such resistance, in both small ways as well as on a grand scale, marks the defining moments of our lives. It is the universal human struggle, and it is through this process that we discover our true nature, come into alignment with our genuine purpose, and feel the simple joy of being alive. But the process is rarely easy or straightforward.

Along the way in our own individual journeys, we are fortunate when we can take inspiration from the personal accounts of those who have confronted enormous obstacles, roadblocks, and detours—in addition to plenty of self-doubt—and yet still found their way home.

Jeremy's story is an extraordinary version of such an account. It is a vibrant, candid, and emotional travelogue of a man whose quest for manhood began much earlier and took far longer than most. What stands out is the author's great compassion for himself and for those around him as he strives toward the most self-evident of truths and the most basic of goals: to be a regular guy.

His book is many things. It is a gift and an offering. It is a fierce battle cry for human rights. It is a testimonial of a series of hard-fought victories, some subtle and others heroic and ultimately transformational. It is the story of a man who found his voice through his body. It is an autobiography of valor and fortitude. It is a poetic statement that sheds the last remaining fibers of the chrysalis from which a new man emerges, proudly and unapologetically, declaring his true identity for all the world to behold.

The evolution of our consciousness begins as we start to de-mystify ourselves to ourselves. It is only through this self-understanding that we can discover the gifts we may bring to others around us. And only by being true to who we are can we unleash the exhilarating potential of our destiny and the wisdom of our soul. The following pages eloquently document such a journey.

Eckhart Tolle writes about our common human longing not only to *be* who we truly are, but also to *be seen* as we truly are. We yearn for the essence of our being to be recognized and acknowledged by our parents and relatives and friends, by our teachers and ministers and coaches, and so too by our physicians. We all share the fundamental need to be respected and loved for the human beings that we are, not merely for the summation of our actions and attributes.

As a whole, our culture is beginning to recognize that an updated, modern definition of health must be broad enough to include more than merely well-controlled blood pressure, low cholesterol, and an absence of joint pain. We now understand that true health must include living in alignment with our core values in an environment that enables their safe expression. Indeed, there is much suffering involved in suppressing or denying our fundamental nature of self, the impulse of our own unique creativity and self-expression, the inspiration and discovery of our passion, our need to connect with others, to feel loved, as well as to love ourselves.

It is not difficult to imagine, given the scope of Jeremy's challenges, that without the loving support and understanding of his parents and siblings and close friends, his story may have had a less happy ending. They too are the heroes of this story and serve as stellar role-models for the loved ones of many others facing the complex predicaments that life often brings, be they gender identity issues or any other myriad topics requiring difficult decisions and uncomfortable conversations. Through both laughter and tears, their roles in Jeremy's life leave an indelible impact on the reader.

In this extraordinary autobiography of an extraordinary man, the central theme is one of acceptance, both of others as well as of ourselves. In reading this book, with its colorful mile markers along the way, the reader is left feeling a connection with the author that resonates with our collective humanity and will help further evaporate the anachronistic smokescreen of prejudice and "other-ness."

David Tusek, M.D.

CHAPTER 1

IT'S A BOY... ER, GIRL?

"A journey of 1000 miles begins with a single step."
— Confucius

In the early summer of 1971 in Southern Michigan, a young couple eagerly awaited the birth of their child. This couple had been high school sweethearts and had already welcomed a daughter, Jayna, three years earlier. Because they were in their mid-twenties, they thought it would be joyous to have another child. So on June 2, out popped a healthy baby...girl? According to my mom, this pregnancy wasn't unusual in any way and everything went according to plan, except my parents thought for sure they were having a boy. Back in the early 1970s, parents had to wait until birth to know whether they had a boy or girl, or rely on old wives tales to determine the sex. Everyone around them thought for sure I was going to be a boy, and in fact, my name was going to be John, after both of my grandfathers. A girl's name was picked out for the "just in case" scenario, which they had to use. I was welcomed into the world as Jennifer Lyn. I'm not sure whether my parents were completely prepared for having another girl and already had my going home outfit, or whether my dad had to run out after my birth, but either way, I thought it was kind of ironic that I went home in a blue dress.

My early years were pretty typical and uneventful. I was fortunate to have been born into an amazing family that loved and supported me, and I wanted for virtually nothing. My parents were patient and gentle with me, even from birth.

As a kid, I definitely struggled. Growing up can be hard for almost anyone, but for me, I struggled with anxiety and depression from a very young age. My mom tirelessly tried to comfort and reassure me that there wasn't anything to fear or worry about, but I couldn't break free from the cycle. I worried about everything and anything, and then I worried when there wasn't anything to worry about. I always had a deep sense that something wasn't right, but I didn't have the vocabulary to try to explain those feelings. I would then get so frustrated when others couldn't understand me. If my family had had ESP, that would've been helpful for all involved.

These issues would always come into play every year at Christmas. I would write a list for Santa a mile long, always filled with sports equipment, Matchbox cars, Star Wars stuff, you name it—whatever toy fad we were currently experiencing. But always traditional "boy" stuff. And year after year, when I would wake up Christmas morning, under the tree would be more than enough.

Typically, my list would be filled, within reason, but after all was opened and barely played with, I would get angry, frustrated, sad, and teary. Decades later, I would understand this better and be able to define it, but back then, I would be mad that the one thing I wanted every day, every year, wasn't there—the thing I was most searching for—the real me.

Stuff couldn't make me happy; it was empty. Nothing stands out more around this Christmas emotional roller coaster than one year when I was about six or seven years old. As tradition would have it, every Christmas Eve, my family, including my aunt, uncle, and cousins, would go over to my paternal grandparents' house for dinner and to exchange gifts. My grandparents' idea of casual was no tie for Grandpa and a pantsuit instead of a blazer and skirt combo for Grandma, so, of course, we put on our best "Christmas casual" as well. For me, this typically meant a dress, brutally painful shoes, and having to shower and comb my hair. My horror at having to wear a dress was always followed by a temper tantrum and endless tugging on anything scratchy. I looked even less comfortable in that garb than did little Idgie in the movie *Fried Green Tomatoes*. Until that fateful Christmas Eve when, among the toys, was a box that I could definitely tell was clothes.

Kids know when they shake or squeeze a box that it has clothes in it, so such boxes are usually tossed aside until the good stuff is opened. The dreadful box of clothes usually meant something pink and scratchy that I would be forced to wear, so I usually hated those boxes, but not this year. Aunt Judy, who must have known me far better than I realized, got me blue corduroys and a T-shirt that looked like a football jersey. It was truly a Christmas miracle. Never have I been so happy to see clothes. I couldn't wait to try them on, and thankfully, I had already made my entrance in that dress, so my mom let me change out of it. What's even better is that this moment was caught in a photograph. The smile on my face is actually genuine.

Looking back, though, I have to say I was so lucky. So my mom made me wear dresses occasionally; so what? She was only doing her best with what was presented in front of her. Year after year, she did her best to balance things out by letting me "be me" as much as possible. I played ice hockey with the boys, rode a mongoose BMX bike around the neighborhood with a matching racing jersey, played T-ball in the summer, rode dirt bikes with my dad, you name it. My childhood wasn't that much different from any other middle-class boy growing up in the '70s. The only exception being that I had a girl's body. Having longer hair wasn't that big of a deal back then; heck, my older cousin Jim had longer hair than I did, and he was super cool. Every time I would play with my friends and would reenact something from TV, or make up some story, my "go to" make-believe name was always Steve. I'm not sure whether I picked it up from the character Steve Austin on the *Six Million-Dollar Man* TV show, or it was just a cool '70s name, but I never pretended to be a female character or chose a girl's name. I knew that didn't fit. Still, no offense to any Steves out there, but I'm glad I outgrew that name.

Another persona I created was an epic Western character named Gunson. I have no idea where that name came from, but it stuck. So on a trip out West one summer in the mid-70s, I got myself all decked out in jeans, cowboy boots, jean jacket, and an awesome coonskin cap. I was the shit that summer! For the entire trip, everyone was to call me Gunson. You could find me out near the campsite hunting chipmunks, or searching for real Indian treasures. Both eluded me.

My entire childhood, I can honestly say that I thought I was a boy. My neighborhood friends were boys; I dressed like one most days, and I copied my dad any chance I could. And just like the other boys in school, I perfected my spitting and swearing in the fifth grade. In fact, I became so good at spitting that one time I accidentally spit in the house on the carpet; there was no recovering from that since my mom saw me do it.

I was always much more comfortable in the boy role. Any time I was reminded that I wasn't male, I would get really angry. I would go from calm to pissed off in thirty seconds flat. I'm not entirely sure what would set me off, but when it happened…look out! A lot of times, the catalyst was when I was unable to do something.

Not in the way of being told I couldn't do or have something, but in hitting my limitations. My dad and I would be playing catch in the yard or playing hockey in the basement, and if I kept missing the ball or puck, I would lash out at my dad and blame him, as if it were his fault I had missed because of a bad throw or shot. When in actuality, I had just missed the ball or puck. For some reason, I took everything so personally, believing because I wasn't a boy, I was less than since a boy would have made that shot. Not the most sound logic. This scenario happened more than I want to admit, and that my dad continued to play with me was a true testament to what an awesome guy he was, and still is. My family basically walked on eggshells around me, hoping they wouldn't poke the bear.

Much later in life, I figured out a lot of the reasons why I would get angry—not all of them—but I'm getting closer. If any of my perceived limitations were because of my gender or they brought to light that I was the wrong gender, my anger and tantrums were triggered. Or more accurately, anytime I realized I wasn't just like my dad or I wouldn't grow up to be a man like him, I would get pissed. Unfortunately, I would take it out on him more times than not. It was almost as if I were jealous that he got to be a man and I didn't. I was devastated that I wasn't his son.

What I didn't realize until transitioning—by which I mean my mental and physical change from being a man trapped in a female body to physically being a man as well—is that I was and always will be his son. What proved that the most was a couple of years into my transition, my parents decided to move to Hawaii to fulfill their own dreams. At that time, my parents and my older sister, Jayna, and her family all lived in Las Vegas, and we probably needed a break from one another. Before they moved, my dad came over to my house, most likely to help me fix something, and on this visit, he had a rifle case with him. This was not just any rifle, but the one that had belonged to his grandfather; my great-grandfather had given it to his son, my grandpa, as a boy, and then it was given to my dad when he was a boy. I thought my dad was going to ask whether he could leave it at my house instead of moving it since it was valuable and meaningful to my dad. Instead, he took the gun out of the case and said to me, as his words caught in his throat, "As tradition would have it, I am now passing this on to my son." Yep, there were tears, and we did that manly hug with big pats on the back. That rifle will always be one of my most prized possessions as well as one of my rites of passage as a man.

As I've said, my childhood was not the typical "girl" experience. Many of you who are in your forties or better may remember Silly Foam. It was basically kids soap in a can like shaving cream, and the metal cans had images of superheroes or various other characters on them. The character's mouth was where the foam came out. I'm sure this foam was a clever ploy from some company to get kids to stop bitching about having to take a bath. Frankly, it was genius. My sister wasn't into Silly Foam as much as I was, but she did have a can of Wonder Woman. Mine, of course, was Superman or Batman. It was awesome, and I would have foam from head to toe in the bathtub. But most of all, I loved it because I used to pretend to shave with it. I would watch my dad shave in the mirror and, of course, mimic him. Once he even gave me an old metal razor with the blade removed to play with; I would douse my face with gobs of foam and proceed to shave my foamy beard and mustache. Naturally, I would shave my entire face, including my forehead, but you get the idea. There's nothing like being a little kid standing next to your dad and shaving in the mirror, grinning from ear to ear.

Thinking back, my dad and I did so many father and son things together, even from a very early age. I vaguely remember riding on his lap when he mowed the lawn. I say vaguely because I usually fell asleep, but I was always eager to go when he asked, just to spend time with him. Around the fifth grade, we moved to the outskirts of our small town and lived in the middle of twenty acres of woods. With all that land, my dad built a few deer hunting blinds up in the trees for rifle and bow hunting seasons. He wasn't a mighty hunter by any means, but he would go every year with a group of guys, mostly to get some guy time away from his family. Only once do I remember him bringing a deer home, and based on our reaction, it was his last. He had hung the deer carcass in our garage, but before he had a chance to tell us, my sister and I walked out there and saw it, creating quite the screams and nightmares. Unfortunately, I did scream like a little girl. After that incident, I'm sure my dad thought it would be easier to miss the shot. I can still see that dead deer staring at me as if it were yesterday.

Even with that visual, I still wanted to go hunting with my dad—of course, not to kill anything, just to hang out with him. We would get up really early while it was still dark, put the coffee and hot chocolate in the thermoses, bundle up in our camouflage gear, and head out with our bow and arrows. I didn't get to go during rifle season mostly because my dad was too worried I would get shot, but more accurately, he was probably afraid I would shoot him. So just as the sun was barely peeking out, we would "quietly" trudge through the woods and climb up the tree to the blind. His simple directions were to sit quietly and wait for the deer. It's pretty safe to say we never saw a lot of deer. Typically, I would have started whispering after about thirty seconds in the blind, then have to drink my hot chocolate, and then, of course, have to go to the bathroom. Repeat that sequence a few more times and that was our day of hunting. Awesome. Not once did my dad tell me to stop talking or get frustrated. He must've enjoyed the simple pleasure of hanging out with me as much as I did with him. After a few hours of daylight and freezing our butts off, we would trek back to the house to tell my mom all about our amazing hunting adventures and how we almost got a deer. Years later, we stopped taking the bows and opted for cameras, all with the same results.

Over the years, hunting gave way to motorcycles and other various sports in the backyard. Somehow, my dad and I usually figured out how to take a seemingly safe activity or sport and tweak it just enough to where we both knew not to tell mom. One of our better ideas one winter was to combine skiing with three-wheeling. It seemed simple enough. We tied a water-ski rope tow to the back of our three-wheeler, and then I put on my downhill skis. Ta-dah! As I mentioned before, we lived out in the middle of nowhere so we had lots of room to roam. So out we went, my dad hauling ass through the woods on the three-wheeler, pulling me behind as I hung onto the rope for dear life. It was awesome! Until the neighbor's dog decided to get in on the fun and chase me down. I'm sure my mom could hear my screams flying through the woods, but other than that, I was grinning ear to ear.

Growing up, I just hung out with my dad like most typical fathers and sons do. Spending that time with him gave me a great opportunity to take in how guys acted and what kind of crazy stuff they did. I copied everything he did, which I'm sure he knew. In fact, one Halloween when I was in the seventh or eighth grade, we had identical costumes. We dressed up as monkeys; we each wore a chimpanzee mask and rubber hands and matching shirts, ties, and blazers. I was his monkey Mini-Me. And naturally, we took that show on the road; my entire family went out to eat at a nice steakhouse, all of us in costume. I think we were the only ones dressed up and we got a lot of looks, but none of us cared, especially me, because I got to be just like my dad. And while that mask was on, everyone assumed we were a father and son, so I never wanted to take that mask off.

CHAPTER 2

CHANGE IS BREWING

"You must always remember…you are braver than you believe, stronger than you seem and smarter than you think."

— Christopher Robin

My growing up years, living at home, were for the most part, uneventful. Or at least nothing majorly scarring happened that would bog me down in therapy as an adult, barring the transgender thing. However, as I got older, I always felt so out of place in my body and in the world. I never felt settled or grounded, even at night when I was trying to sleep. I was always so tense throughout my body that I can only describe it as feeling like I slept on my bed instead of in it. I never let myself relax enough to sink into the mattress, as if I were constantly on guard, waiting for something to happen. It would take me hours to fall asleep, but when I finally drifted off, I was dead to the world—so much so that I was a bedwetter up until I was fourteen years old. I debated whether or not even to mention this situation, but what the hell—if I'm going to be truthful and air my dirty laundry, why pick and choose?

Being a bedwetter and for so long was embarrassing and very isolating. After doctors' visits, bladder tests, bed alarms, and the like, I was finally told I would just grow out of it someday. But waiting for that day was painful and frustrating to say the least. I missed out on a lot of things like going to sixth grade camp and sleepovers with friends. I had to make up tons of stories about why I couldn't spend the night somewhere, and people either thought I was a very sickly child or not very friendly. Of course, neither was true. But that experience gave me a chance to perfect my lying skills, which I honed as an adult. Thankfully, I stopped wetting the bed the summer before my freshman year of high school, so I was able to go to band camp. Band camp was not much of a prize, but it was a big accomplishment for me.

For a long time, I didn't have the vocabulary to describe adequately my feelings and emotions, and it was really confusing to have my identity, or the way I perceived myself, be the complete opposite of how I looked. Being transgender is not an easy thing to describe to someone, including myself, and at that time, I had never even heard the term. I just thought I was crazy. Today, knowing what I know now, I have a pretty good grasp on being transgender and what that means, but to describe it as being a man born into a woman's body, while truthful, is far too vague and benign. There is way more to it, and a lot of the time, trying to understand and accept it has been emotionally, mentally, and physically painful and all consuming. Growing up is hard enough; try adding this crap on top. No matter where I went or what I did, I was always with me, and I could never escape.

At times, I would emulate my sister and try to act more like a girl, but it always felt foreign and awkward. Mostly, I wanted to do the things Jayna did because I just wanted to be around her. My thinking was that to play with her and her friends, I had to be "one of them" or I would get kicked out of the club. I remember one time when I was about eight or nine, Jayna got a Barbie that she could apply makeup to and style the hair. It was a life-size Barbie head that, just below the shoulders, turned into a plastic tray to hold the makeup and stuff. Well, I thought I wanted one too, and I got it. Jayna would spend hours making her Barbie bust look perfect. Mine, not so much. My Barbie head looked like she had the makings of dreadlocks because I never combed the hair, and instead of using the included makeup, I decided she needed something a bit stronger. I used permanent marker! My lady looked more like she was heading into battle with her war paint on.

I always tried so hard to give girly things a try, hoping to enjoy them as much as my sister did, but they always backfired. Lucky for me, though, Jayna never kicked me out of her group; rather, she included me in everything. She and all of her friends let me tag along no matter what, almost like I was a little mascot to the group. In my hometown, we only had three schools—elementary was grades one through four, middle school was five through eight, and high school was for grades nine through twelve. Since Jayna was three years older than me, each year I was the "baby" of the school, she was also in that building. So when I moved up to middle school as a fifth grader, Jayna was the grown up eighth grader who let me sit with her entourage at lunch if I needed to. I didn't appreciate that gesture until I hit high school. As a shy, depressed, and fearful kid, it was a lifeline to have my big sister in the same building all day long and know I always had a familiar face waiting for me at lunchtime.

But feeling disjointed was always a constant underlying hum to my life, and to be honest, it still is on my mind more than it should be. But as I write this book, I am reliving so many experiences and emotions and finally gaining closure. I'm sure part of the reason for having my transgender status in the forefront of my mind most days is because I have been living a stealth (secret or not "out") lifestyle for the last six years, and now with the publication of this book and my story, I am about to embark on living completely out loud.

Looking back, there were definite clues of what was to come. As I matured, I started looking at my life differently. I never dated in high school, and my only experience with "going with" anyone was in the fifth grade. And that was awkward because it was with a boy. To me it was like hanging out with a buddy, but he thought differently and wanted to hold my hand and kiss me. I was not a fan of those activities. Talk about uncomfortable, but that's what I assumed a girl was supposed to do. Fortunately, I was busy enough with ice-skating and hockey that I didn't have time to repeat that boy-girl nonsense. My crushes, if I had them, were typically reserved for my female teachers. I've always been a fan of the older ladies. By high school, my friends were dating and doing the typical teenage boy-girl stuff while I concentrated on playing hockey and hanging out with a couple of safe friends. Many times, I lied and claimed that I did things like dated so-and-so, mostly to fit in and get people to stop asking me questions. However, I'm proud of myself that I only lied about it instead of actually doing something I wasn't ready for, just to fit in.

Mostly, I was terrified and extremely confused. The thought of any sexual experience with a boy was so foreign and scary to me. I hated that I was even perceived as a girl, had girl parts, and that a boy would find me attractive. It didn't make sense to me since I saw myself as one of the guys. At the time, I didn't really have any of those feelings toward women either, mostly because I was just trying to figure myself out and would suppress any real feelings that came up. And again, without having any knowledge of being transgender, I couldn't figure this out.

The summer before my freshman year, I got my first period. Most girls at school had already had theirs, but being a late bloomer was a good thing for me; I managed to make it to fourteen before getting mine. On that fateful morning, I went to the bathroom as usual, but this time there was blood in the toilet and on the toilet paper when I wiped. I screamed for my mom because, naturally, I thought I was bleeding to death. When she came flying into the bathroom, thinking something awful had happened, she was relieved that it was just my period, but I was freaked out. My mom was great and calmed me down somewhat, enough to explain what was really going on and walk me through what I needed to do. Obviously, I wasn't as clueless as it may seem; I knew full well what was happening, but I was in denial. This wasn't supposed to happen to me. How could my body continue to betray me?

This felt like the beginning of the end, so around this time, I truly began my battle with depression. The only positive is that going forward, I rarely had a period. It was hit and miss, and not uncommon for me to have only three or four a year. Over the years, I've had medical tests, ultrasounds, and whatnot, and at first, doctors said it was due to my small size and being extremely physically active. Later, another doctor said that only one of my ovaries was working, while another doctor, much later, wasn't even sure I had two ovaries. You may be wondering, "How could you not know?" Truth is I never asked, and now I don't want to know.

When I was seven, I'd had a hernia repair operation, so I have a small scar right where my right ovary supposedly is. That doctor, who thought I missed so many periods, said it was my right ovary that might not be functioning. And the doctor, who said I might not have both, mentioned this during a physical exam when she was unable to feel the right ovary. I'm not claiming anything here. I take my parents' word for it that the small round mass that was removed was a hernia and nothing else. But I would be remiss if I didn't say I wonder whether I had an undescended testicle removed. Even though I wonder, I don't want to know because everything in my life has happened for a reason. Part of me wants to hang onto that possibility while the other part is afraid it isn't true. I look at it as my having taken the scenic route to manhood, and I wouldn't change a thing.

Once I got to high school, every year in the fall, we were required to have a sports physical before we could play school sports, and I played on the varsity men's ice hockey team. "Why did you play on the men's team?" you ask. Well, back then, there weren't any girls teams in the area, so I always played with the boys. I was good enough to continue to play hockey at the varsity level, so the school let me on the team. I know it pissed off a few of my teammates, but they were probably intimidated that I was a better skater than they were. They got over it pretty quickly once we hit the ice. So to be able to play, I had to get that physical, and every year I would panic and make my mom actually call the doctor's office to confirm that a Pap smear was not part of a sports physical. It may seem crazy that I even thought about a Pap smear, but as my body changed during puberty, I knew it was something that would eventually have to happen, and in my worrisome head, any trip to the doctor could be that day. I was so neurotic about it that I made my mom call while I was in the room and could hear the conversation—just to make sure she really did it. My mom was a trooper, as was the staff at the doctor's office. None of them made fun of me for asking every single year. And for anyone reading this who may not be familiar with what a Pap smear is, well, it's a horrific experience where a doctor physically has to check out the inside of your lady business. I say horrific because it's super uncool and embarrassing when you feel like you shouldn't have an "inny" in the first place. What I wouldn't have given to have had a prostate exam instead. Any rational person would know that a Pap smear is never part of the sports physical, but one can never be too sure. Since I was this fanatical about avoiding that experience, you can probably imagine my thoughts and horror around having sex with a guy. It was best just to avoid dating altogether for as long as I could.

But all of my clever avoidance of my incorrect and confusing genitalia ended one fateful day. To get right to it, I had had some burning when I went to the bathroom, which lasted much longer than it should have, but when the itching started, I finally had to tell someone. It was like I had sat on a nest of fire ants and could pee fire. The pain was excruciating, and for someone who wanted to forget that she had female genitalia, this made it impossible. All of my attention was focused on that area. FYI, scratching may help in the moment, but I think the real reason people say not to is because once you've really scratched and roughed up that tender skin, the hot shower and lotion stings like a bitch. I tried to ignore the burning but to no avail, so when I finally told my mom, she came back with that dreaded phrase, "Do you want me to look at it?" Now don't get all weird; that's what moms do, and of course, I didn't want her to look at it. I didn't want anyone to look at it, ever. But the burning and itching got so bad that we had to go to urgent care.

My mom and I sat in the lobby, she quietly reading a ten-year-old magazine, me squirming in the chair and sweating. Another FYI, sweating doesn't help that situation either. My biggest fear was that the doctor was going to do more than just look, so I begged my mom to tell the doctor just to prescribe some medication and take my word for it. And again her being the trooper that she was, she did make that request, but we both knew the doctor would decide differently. Now if you ask me, my mom could've been more persuasive and forceful to help me get out of it, but unfortunately, the doctor said I would definitely need a pelvic exam and Pap smear. My worst fear was coming true. And what I wanted to shout was, "Hell no! Boys don't get those procedures done!" But, of course, I said nothing and started to cry. I was scared, humiliated, and embarrassed. My mom knew this; she knew me better than I knew myself, and she said it was up to me whether I wanted to go ahead and have this done, but she assured me the pain and itching would only get worse. It was hard to imagine it getting any worse.

We sat in the waiting area so I could think about it. Every female doctor, nurse, and receptionist there was awesome and understood this decision was difficult for me. My mom and I sat there for what seemed like days, going from silence to talking about how long it would take, what they were going to do, and how I would feel better once it was over. The receptionist at the check-in desk even came out a couple of times to check on and reassure me. That would've been more helpful if she hadn't been an old neighbor of ours while I was younger, and the mom of a kid I was in band with. Of course, I would know somebody at the doctor's office during this horrific and private time; that was just my luck. After much deliberation and, more importantly, the itching intensifying due to my nervousness, I decided it was time to go ahead with the exam. My mom went in the room with me for support. I got changed into the paper gown, but I left my socks on so I wouldn't be naked. Funny how keeping your socks on actually helps.

And then it got worse. Now imagine having a stranger hunker down between your legs with a headlamp and tools. What I wouldn't have given for an out-of-body experience at that moment, but again, I was not that lucky. The doctor was as quick and gentle as she possibly could have been, but my embarrassment and fear overshadowed the situation. To say that it was uncomfortable is an understatement; it flat out hurt. And here's the real kicker—

after all that trauma, we left with a prescription for antibiotics and a topical cream. Isn't that what I had originally asked for hours earlier while my pants were still on? If they had just taken my word for it! After that day, I was different. For most young girls, their first pelvic exam isn't life-changing, but for me, it meant I could no longer deny that I had a female's body.

At times, I could almost forget I had a female body, but when I did get a period or had another exam, reality came crashing down. During those times when I could forget, I would do things that would reinforce my chosen gender identity. I would swipe my mom or sister's eyebrow pencil and draw on a mustache and/or beard just to see how I would look. Sorry to both of them for making them think they were going through those pencils like hotcakes. I would spend a lot of time in the bathroom staring at my fake facial hair and trying out all kinds of manly poses and facial expressions. For a moment, I felt better, even normal. My family will probably be relieved to find out why I spent so much time in the bathroom.

After puberty set in, I had to be more creative in front of the bathroom mirror so I wouldn't see the terrible new addition to my body…my boobs. Those definitely brought out my true body dysphoria for sure. With my mustache and beard drawn on, from the shoulders up, I could see a boy looking back at me in the mirror. And even with certain clothes on, I could almost make that girl disappear. But catching a glimpse of myself in the mirror when I was changing or getting in or out of the shower was devastating. I don't think I can put into words how much it hurt and disgusted me to see a female body with a boy's face on it. I spent the next few decades avoiding all mirrors, learning to ignore my reflection, and when I did use the mirror to get ready in the morning, I perfected my self-hatred by honing in on all of my features I hated.

Intertwined with self-loathing and staying ultra busy with hockey and playing percussion in the band, I managed to do really well in school. Fortunately, school always came easy to me, and I am truly grateful. Good thing too because I spent too much time with my mind elsewhere or being completely "checked out." Because of my grades, I was in the National Honor Society and was accepted to many different colleges around the U.S. I was even offered scholarships to play women's ice hockey at Harvard and Colby College, but I turned down both of those opportunities. I told everyone else it was because I didn't want to go to school back East, but the real truth was that I didn't want to leave home. I was still struggling with finding myself and battling depression, so I wasn't ready to be on my own. For some reason, I couldn't admit the truth, so I made up excuses and lies about why I didn't want to go away to college, probably fooling no one. To each college acceptance letter that came in, I said, "No," even to the University of Colorado, which oddly enough I later attended and graduated from. But at eighteen, I needed to stay closer to home and figure out myself, if possible.

My first college experience, and I say "experience" lightly, didn't even last a week. I attended Michigan State University just like my parents had. Growing up a Spartan fan, smack dab in the middle of Michigan Wolverine country, made for a great rivalry during football season. I went to freshman orientation the summer before school started, and I managed to survive three days away from home with complete strangers. My stomach was a wreck and I didn't sleep. I skipped the meals because I was too shy to ask whether I could sit with people I didn't know. Those three days sucked, but since I had made it, it went in the win category. When it was actually time to go to school in the fall, I had worked myself up into a nice frenzy. My mom and I walked the campus to make sure I knew where all my classes were; that was one stress that could be checked off the list.

But the biggest stress of all was moving into the dorms. Sometimes universities over-enroll students, which means they put three freshmen in one dorm room. Dorm rooms are barely big enough for two; you can imagine how comfy it was for three. My parents and I trudged to my room with a shitload of stuff, opened the door, and found out that not only would three of us be in that room for a year, but I was the last one to move in. The other two girls were high school friends, which definitely made me the odd man out—in more ways than one. It also looked as if they had moved in weeks ago. The room was packed to the brim with their stuff and filthy. Perfect. Some of their crap was even on what was to be my bed. According to my mom, my eyes were huge and all the blood drained from my face, leaving a slight greenish hue to it. What looked like a pile of clothes on one of the beds turned out to be my roommate, dead asleep in the afternoon. The only reason I knew that girl wasn't dead was because she looked up briefly when we opened the door to give me a look that said, "What the fuck do you want?" This was going well.

My parents and I quickly and quietly made my bed, put some clothes in the 1/8th of the closet that was left, and got the hell out of there. School wasn't starting for a couple of more days, so I decided to ride back with my parents and spend the night at home since we didn't live that far away. The car ride home was pretty quiet. I didn't say anything and my parents chatted among themselves. They were pretty intuitive folks, or I was just super-easy to read, but they knew I was scared shitless. That's got to be a tough moment for parents—to see their kid so frightened and not know whether they should push the child out of the nest or hold her back. It was clear I just needed more time to grow up and become less afraid of the world.

When it was time to go back to school because classes were starting, I couldn't do it. Just shy of having an actual panic attack, I broke down and said I didn't want to go back. Thankfully, my parents understood and were awesome; that was all I had needed to say. Not once was I made to feel I had failed or that they were disappointed in me. Those feelings didn't come from them, but I sure thought that of myself. I beat myself up about it for a long time. So instead of driving up to Michigan State for classes, we drove up to get my stuff out of that shithole room. So that was the start of my college career. The next day, I enrolled at Washtenaw Community College and spent the next two years living at home, slowly gaining the nerve to leave. My apprehension about leaving home resulted from my feeling that everything about me was disjointed and I couldn't make sense of how I fit in the world. I was depressed and had little, if any, self-esteem. I was almost crippled by fear, and the only way I knew how to cope was to stay at home in my safe zone.

As I finished up my first semester at the community college, I was feeling better about myself and was making great strides with my self-esteem. We headed into the winter break, and I was actually excited to resume my studies in January. All of that changed on December 18th. Early that morning, around 1 or 2 a.m., the phone rang. Because my dad owned the town grocery store, we were used to calls in the middle of the night, usually the alarm company or something to that effect, and I typically slept right through them. Not this time. For some reason, when I heard my dad pick up the phone, I jumped out of bed to find out who it was. No clue why I did that. I went to my parents' room, and that's when my life changed. The call was from my uncle Jim; my oldest cousin, Jim, had died in a car accident. I froze. I couldn't do anything, no tears, nothing. We sat up at the kitchen table for hours in disbelief. I could not wrap my head around this news. My cousin Jim was six years older than me, and I had looked up to him as an older brother my whole life. To me, this guy could do no wrong; he was the epitome of cool, and I wanted to be just like him. He was the guy I emulated, and I envisioned that if I had been born a boy, I would have looked just like him. I had put this guy on a pedestal. I can remember hanging out in my cousins' basement, watching Jim and his friends play pool or just hang out. I did everything possible to be around him whenever I had the chance, and I'm sure I was a pest or in the way, but he never made me feel unwanted. He always included me the best he could, but unfortunately, he saw me as this little girl, and once I hit puberty, I was almost embarrassed to be around him. I can't say that he and I were super close near the end, but I wish he had known how much I adored him.

Once daylight came, my parents and I went over to my aunt and uncle's house. It would be the first time I saw my dad cry. It was the most gut-wrenching day I had experienced, and we all appeared to be numb and motionless. The house filled up quickly with Jim's friends, and everyone came together to provide some sort of comfort. This death was all too sudden, and I hated it. I kept waiting to wake up from the nightmare and go back to a normal life that included Jim, but that never happened. It took me a while to show any emotion, and I didn't break down until I was back in my own home. Expressing any emotion at all was extremely difficult for me, especially crying in front of people. Losing Jim was a devastating blow to our entire family, and there has been a hole ever since.

When it was time to head back to classes in January, my self-confidence and self-assuredness were gone. I went right back to my old ways and found myself again crippled by fear. I was now afraid to drive to school and worried about the snow and ice like never before. My fear was so destructive that I ended up dropping all but two classes that semester. I couldn't get myself together, but I didn't know why. In hindsight, I can say with confidence that I didn't really take the time to grieve for Jim because I wanted to have an outward appearance that I was okay, like I always did—never letting anyone know I was hurting. And I also didn't realize how deep his loss would affect me. I had lost someone whom I idolized—the man I imagined I would grow up to be like.

By the time I received my Associates degree, after being on the extended plan, I had decided I was mostly ready to move out, but not completely on my own. My sister was living in Tucson, so I transferred out to the University of Arizona and ended up living off-campus with her. I know I wasn't really on my own, but it was true progress in my book. After one semester there, just long enough to choose my anthropology major and to build up my confidence a bit, I decided I actually wanted to go to college someplace I liked. The only reason I had picked Arizona was because my sister lived there, but when things in her life changed, we both decided a change of venue was in order.

As I mentioned before, when I was in high school I had applied to and been accepted at the University of Colorado in Boulder. The idea of the Rocky Mountains was still intriguing to me, and I was finally ready to give it a shot. So my parents, sister, and I took a quick roadtrip to check out Boulder and CU. The school was just as awesome as I had imagined, and since I had already been accepted a few years earlier, the registrar's office let me fill out an application on the spot and welcomed me to the school. The only catch to being accepted only two months before the start of the fall semester was that very few classes were still open, and I would have to take night classes. No problem. And because this time around my sister was coming with me, I got to continue to live off campus and bypass the dorm experience. So for the next couple of years, while I finished up my degree, my sister gave me the courage and security I needed to live away from home. She was literally my rock, and because of the circumstances in her own life, I hope I was the same to her as well.

At CU, I had the chance to play college hockey, even if it were only a club sport and I was on the girls' team. This would be the first time I had ever played hockey with girls, so it was weird. I never felt at home on the ice playing with women, so I kept to myself, making up excuses and lies why I couldn't hang out with the team. I have to admit, I was a total hermit during my CU college days, so I didn't come away with lasting friendships, typical college memories, or even good stories to tell, but for me, it was enough.

As I was getting ready to graduate from CU, my sister Jayna, who had gone to college in Hawaii, was at a point where she was ready to get on with her own life and stop taking care of me. She missed Hawaii and knew it was time to go back and find new adventures. I was proud of her for taking care of herself, and I knew this was the right decision for her, but again, I was afraid to be alone. What the hell was wrong with me? Why was I so afraid to grow up, be an adult, and live on my own? Well, there was nothing wrong with me; however, I had learned to let fear shape my life.

Now that I was graduating from college, I still felt like I had no direction. Choosing anthropology as a major was interesting and fun, but not exactly the most useful. So after talking with a friend who was a massage therapist, I decided to go to massage school. I'm sure my parents were just thrilled that after they had paid for me to go to college, I wanted to do something totally unrelated and even had the nerve to ask for help in paying for it. But as usual, my parents supported me and made that happen. Off to massage school I went, and it proved to be a life-changing experience. In fact, massage school ended up being one of the most important times in my life. It was a year of self-help and exhausting inner work, all while learning a new skill set. I made some amazing connections and friendships; I finally had my "college" experience. Including learning how to drink like a fish.

As more and more of my personal demons started to bubble to the surface, like depression and actually "feeling" emotions, I began numbing myself with alcohol. This was the first time I had started drinking and pretty soon, I had made up for lost time and was known as the one who would need to have help getting home. I drank myself into a deep depression, and midway through the school year, I became suicidal. Getting bodywork every day and being in a safe environment among friends, it was difficult not to experience changes, good or bad. I had heard a statistic that a lot of marriages or relationships don't last through massage school, and I could clearly see why. It was like a yearlong therapy retreat. And through that process, I started the journey straight and came out gay, even though I really hadn't dated anyone.

A lot of the inner turmoil that erupted that year came from my realization that I was attracted to women, more specifically one of my teachers. I think it was the first time that I was truly attracted to someone and had all those stupid things like butterflies in my stomach when she walked in the room, stuttering when I tried to say something to her; I looked and sounded like a complete idiot.

But it scared me that I was feeling all these things about a woman. It finally felt right that I would be involved with a woman, but what did this mean? Of course, it would make sense that a man would fall for a woman; the problem was that the man was buried underneath a woman's body. Would I even have a shot? Was I okay with or ready to be gay? I agonized and worried and finally talked with some friends, all of whom were very supportive and helped me to deal with and accept myself. Having to deal with my sexuality alone was, at times, the reason why I didn't want to live. It felt too big, too difficult. How do I tell my family? Will they accept me? As it turned out, I worried way too much because, as usual, things worked out.

The Christmas before my graduation from massage school, my parents came out to Boulder to visit, and once again, these poor folks listened and watched their kid struggle. I took them out for Chinese one night and dropped the bomb on them that I was gay. They didn't even flinch; they just hugged me and reassured me that I was loved. Yes, I do know how lucky and blessed I am to have them. I think the most difficult part of the evening was my other news—that I had a drinking problem and was in AA. While they were supportive with that too, I would imagine news of your child struggling with alcohol would be harder for a parent to hear. Just my guess.

After graduation, I began dating the teacher whom I had lusted after the entire year prior. We were together on and off for almost two years, and while the relationship didn't last, it was a pivotal one for me—one where I learned a lot about myself, what I wanted, and what I didn't want. And most importantly, how to or not to date a woman. Sorry, guys; I don't have a lot of words of wisdom on that except to say that women are really hard to figure out.

So why all this backstory? Well, it's all part of my foundation. Becoming a massage therapist and going through a difficult breakup is how I landed in Las Vegas. By the time my first relationship imploded, my sister had been living in Las Vegas and was getting ready to open up her first haircare franchise. She knew I was floundering and was hurting, so she said, "Come on down to Vegas for the summer; I'll take good care of you." What's funny is that I ended up getting an amazing job as a massage therapist at the Hard Rock Hotel and made way more money than she did that summer, so I was able to take good care of her.

Most days working at the hotel spa were fun, but harder work than I expected. Schlepping a massage table out to the pool area in the Vegas summer—not fun. And to massage some drunken asshole, well even better. What made it tolerable were those drunks usually tipped really well. Either they had a ton of money or were too drunk to notice what they had given me; either way, it worked out well. Over the course of that summer working full-time, I gave more massages than I had in the last year combined.

I worked on every personality and body type possible. Whenever I massaged smaller guys, I found myself staring and comparing myself to them. I'm sure that sounds kind of strange, and when I realized what I was doing, I thought it was strange too and a bit disturbing. In fact, the first time I noticed myself doing it, it almost made me shit my pants. Why was I checking these guys out? Sometimes when I was working on their hands, usually when they were asleep, I would measure my hand size to theirs and think to myself, "Hmmm, we are about the same size in stature and hands and feet; I wonder whether I could pull off being a guy?" Sorry to any short guy out there who may have received a massage from me that summer. I was working on my own stuff, so I'm sure the quality of my massages sucked. Or, hopefully, you were one of those drunk guys who didn't notice. That Vegas summer in 1996 was the first time I became aware of the term "transgender" and what that meant. I didn't know anyone who was transgender, but from Internet searches, I came across the term and dove into learning anything I could. I even entertained the thought of making a change myself. Thoughts always ended with, "I can't." But the next question to myself was always, "Can I live the rest of my life as is?"

After that summer, I went back to Boulder and pretended everything was fine. I never really found my groove, so about a year or so later, I found myself back in Las Vegas. I worked at different spas, and again I would drift off into my own inner dialogue, trying to figure things out. While I know I have always been transgender, I was able to suppress it for a long time and almost convince myself otherwise.

At times, I would try to dive into the LGBT community and butch it up, which sometimes seemed to help, but I never really embraced it. You'll notice I don't use the term "lesbian" very often, or ever; that is because I never thought of myself that way. At times, I might have been able to say I was gay, but never did I say lesbian; mostly I danced around it altogether. Saying the words out loud, "I'm a lesbian" or "I'm gay," seemed so foreign and untrue because that's not who I was. I was a straight man whom nobody could see.

Other times, I went through spurts where I really tried to embrace being a girl. I would wear makeup and girly clothes, and I would grow my hair out in feminine styles. But during those times, I always felt so out of place. Never did I wear white shirts unless I had a sweater or something over it because I couldn't stand to see or have someone else see that I was wearing a bra. At the time, my sister could never understand that one and would tell me to get over it. She was only reacting to the sister in front of her, not fully realizing the bigger problem. Even when I asked her to do my hair in really girly ways, it was so hard for me to see the end result in the mirror. The color or cut typically came out really well, but deep down, I was afraid that other people might compliment me. What I mean is that even though I worked hard at looking nice, I never wanted someone to call me pretty because I wasn't supposed to be pretty; I was supposed to be handsome.

For so long, it felt like I could never win. On and off, whether or not I was in a girly phase, I would continue to research transgender stuff on the Internet or in bookstores. Of course, at the bookstores I was always nervous that someone would see what I was looking at, so I never bought anything there. I would go home and buy the books online. I would read them, panic that someone might find out that I had the books, and then literally throw them away in the trash. Once they went in the trash bag, I would toss in old food or coffee grounds to cover up the books. My apologies to Loren Cameron and Jamison Green for skewing their book sales numbers. They both probably thought more people were buying their books, which was awesome, but it was the same dumb-ass guy buying and throwing them away. Can you imagine the look on the person's face who found those books in the dumpster?

Transition is just that—a transition in thinking, beliefs, and attitude, in addition to physicality. Over the years, it was becoming increasingly difficult for me to stuff these thoughts and desires away, until finally I had to come to terms with my options and make a decision. It was time.

CHAPTER 3

FINDING THE COURAGE TO JUMP

"Nothing happens until the pain of staying the same outweighs the pain of change."

— Arthur Burt

As I briefly mentioned in the last chapter, for most of my life I have struggled with and battled depression in various degrees, have isolated myself, and at times, have been suicidal. Wow, what an uplifting way to begin a chapter! For many reading this book, whether you are transgender yourself or someone close to you is, suicide is a relevant topic to your life. It was something I had to deal with before I could fully transition. Transgender people are some of the most courageous and inspiring people I know, but even with all that strength, feelings of hopelessness and despair exist. Even the bravest transgender people are still human, and at times, they think they don't have what it takes. They feel they can't do it, and they get bogged down in the "what ifs" and fear of not belonging. What makes us courageous is sticking it out and making a drastic change in our lives, no matter the consequences. Before I realized that, I thought I was weak and crazy, and a viable option was to give up.

During my junior year of high school, I had my first suicidal thoughts, and ideations of committing suicide consumed my mind. At that time, I didn't have the maturity or the knowledge to understand why I was depressed; I just knew I didn't feel like I fit in and that I never would, so it made sense to me to take myself out of the equation. I remember once saying to my parents that I wished I had a drug problem so I could go to rehab. Crazy, huh? What I was really thinking was at least a drug problem would give me a reason why I felt like shit. I knew a few people in high school who had gone to rehab, and everyone rallied and supported them. When they came back to school, they seemed better, like they had a sense of purpose. Deep down, maybe what I was really craving was the rally and support; who knows? But what I missed was, in the midst of that depression, I was getting the rally and support, but I couldn't see it.

My mom later told me that when I would leave the house in the morning to drive myself to school, which was about a thirty-minute trip, she would call the school to let the counselor know what time I left and approximately when I should arrive. Once my first class, chemistry, started, another teacher, would come in the back of our classroom through a door that adjoined to hers, tap me on the head because I was usually asleep in the back row, smile at me, and leave out the opposite door. Everyone thought she was just taking a shortcut through our classroom, but in actuality, she was checking in on me, and then she would let someone know that I was there safe and sound. Then someone would call my mom to let her know. A variation of this scenario would happen in reverse at the end of the day. To this day, I owe those women, a world of gratitude for going above and beyond, caring and loving me.

At the time, I didn't think anyone had anything to worry about with me, but in reality, every reason existed. I didn't care if I made it to or from school, actually to or from anywhere. I clearly remember seeing how far I could drive to school with my eyes closed. Fortunately, we lived way out in the country and there wasn't any traffic in the morning, but a few times, I narrowly missed some mailboxes. By the grace of God, the only accident I had was spinning out into someone's front yard. It didn't scare me, just embarrassed me. Naturally, I blamed it on the icy roads. This extra work for the staff at school could only go on for so long, and eventually, I was hospitalized in a youth psychiatric facility. I was supposed to be there to get help, but because I was so scared to be away from home, I lied and manipulated my way out in seventy-two hours. The hospital was in Detroit, and I remember when my parents and I drove up, I wasn't sure whether the bars on the windows were to keep the crazies in or keep people out. Either way, I wasn't staying for long.

My introduction to the hospital was a nice strip search in front of a nurse who catalogued all my belongings and then took my belt, shoelaces, and headphones, but left me with my tapes and Walkman. Brilliant. I can honestly say I have never been more terrified than being in that psych ward. For the next seventy-two hours, I barely slept or ate, and my stomach was in knots. Tons of kids my age were there, but I didn't want to know anything about them; I just wanted to get the hell out of there. At every meal, a staff person would sit at the table with us, making sure that nobody stole any of the plastic utensils or anything sharp. They called it being on suicide watch. Seriously? Did they really expect us to slit our wrists with plastic spoons? In the afternoons, I would meet with the psychiatrist, and eventually, I managed to convince him that I was not suicidal and could go home. The rest of the time was spent playing Ping-Pong and making crafts. The place was more like a babysitting service for at risk teens. I stayed long enough to make a nice painted hat, but I missed leatherworking by a day. It would've been funny if they had let patients make leather belts as a parting gift to their stint in the hospital. Money well spent.

Even though I didn't take this hospitalization seriously enough and I bypassed getting help, it did have a lasting effect on me because I never wanted to be back in a place like that again. After that experience, I was able to get my shit together a little better, and thanks to one of my teachers, I found a great therapist. Even with having someone to talk to who was non-partial and objective, I still struggled with talking about my feelings. I didn't share much, and I began to shut off from feeling anything. I'm sure I made it very difficult on this therapist since I wasn't willing to do the work.

Without fully understanding what was going on, I can only describe myself at this time as being numb. I hated myself so badly, and I couldn't stand to look at myself in any way. Closing myself off from feeling anything began to take a toll. I craved feeling something, anything. So I began cutting on my skin. It started out with small nicks on my arms or legs, nothing noticeable, but soon escalated to an overwhelming desire to carve my skin open. It was almost as if by cutting the skin open, I was letting out the pressure inside, and seeing the cut and blood finally gave me a reason to feel sad and angry and experience the pain. I would find all kinds of things to cut my skin with, including Swiss Army knives, screwdrivers, and just about anything that was somewhat sharp. Now I get it why the hospital staff hawked everybody at meals. I would cut on my wrists, but I never had the guts, or God never let my hand move that deep, to put my life in any danger. The cuts were never more than what a Band-Aid could remedy.

I lost the desire to die once I started cutting, but I still needed to feel pain. Maybe I thought I deserved it. Cutting later gave way to tattoos; some of my earliest tattoos are covering up my self-inflicted scars. Once I started getting body art done, I never cut my skin again. Over time, I have done a lot of work on myself to understand why I cut in the first place, and I have no desire to do that again; however, I will admit I still get a rush from the pain of a tattoo.

All through my twenties and thirties, I ebbed and flowed with depression. When it got really bad, I would get myself back on antidepressants or anti-anxiety medications, which would reel me back in enough to function. During those times, I usually headed back into therapy as well, for a psychological tune up. The summer of 2008 was one of those times, and by then, the pull of being in the wrong body and living as the wrong gender was all-consuming. At this time, I had moved back to Las Vegas to go into the haircare business with my dad and sister. And even though we were extremely busy at work, once again, my mind would focus and obsess on not wanting to be me anymore. I hated this life and was exhausted from feeling overwhelmed. I was raised as a Christian, which I still am today, so I prayed constantly for God to help me, to make these thoughts go away, or just to take me home. Only one of these requests was answered.

I didn't realize it at the time, but God's help came in the form of leading me to the right psychotherapist. I didn't know it when I was searching for a therapist, but I landed in the office of someone who was a true transgender advocate. I began meeting with a woman named Jane every week, and for the first month or so, it was just the typical getting to know my backstory and who I was. Same stuff I'd been through with every other therapist in my life. But the difference this time was that I went back into therapy to deal with being transgender, and I was almost sure that I was ready. Each week I became more and more comfortable, yet increasingly nervous. I knew I was in a safe environment where I could finally open up and share my deep, dark feelings.

About two months into therapy, on one extremely hot day in August—it was Vegas after all—I sat in Jane's office, completely bundled up in layers of clothes that included a heavy sweatshirt. I knew when I left my house that I was going to say something out loud for the first time that day, and because of my nervousness, I was freezing. The session started like any other, but I was extremely fidgety, and it didn't take a professional to notice that I had something specific on my mind. I sat there and struggled to get any words out that made sense. All I could say was that I had something I needed to share, something buried deep that I had never spoken about before. I was shaking and sweating so badly that I couldn't decide whether the sweatshirt had been a good idea or not. But this was stress sweat. I could hear my heart beat loudly in my ears, and I could see the beat through my sweatshirt, and now I thought I was going to throw up. Jane never pressured me to say anything; she gently set a wastebasket next to me and said, "Use it if you need it." It felt like it took days to speak, but eventually, I managed to mutter, "I'm not a girl."

That was pretty much it. Just saying that phrase out loud changed my life. Jane's only reaction was, "That's great news.... Thank you for sharing that with me. I'm proud of you." For the first time in my life, I felt relieved and finally knew that I was going to be okay. This was the first time I had actually done real work in therapy and been willing to figure out my real issues. Of course, I had no idea what my new journey was going to entail, but I was ready, or so I thought.

Now that I had come to terms with being transgender—at least well enough to tell one person—the next few months, Jane and I delved much deeper into my thoughts and feelings on this process to determine whether I was ready to make the leap to become the man I knew I was or whether this would be the extent of my journey. It was at this time in therapy that I finally addressed my issues around alcohol and the reasons why I drank too much. By drinking large quantities, I was trying to numb and accept myself and fit in. Since coming out as transgender, I have been able to walk away from alcohol. I still drink from time to time, but it is no longer something I need in my life. For most people, trans or not, the quote at the beginning of the chapter is very relatable. It's true that you have to weigh the pain of change against the pain of staying the same and figure out which is greater. I had come to that moment in my life where if I stayed the same and stuffed my real self down anymore, I wouldn't stay alive, so any change in the direction of transition was infinitely better. It was time to jump.

We talked about the logistics of transition and what that meant, such as hormone therapy and surgeries. Jane was more than willing to write a letter on my behalf, as is required, to be able to start receiving hormones, have surgeries, or even change personal documents. According to the World Professional Association for Transgender Health (WPATH), all gender questioning individuals must follow a Standards of Care protocol. It used to mean that someone had to live full time, for one year, as his or her chosen gender before being able to receive hormone therapy, but fortunately, things have changed. Or at least there are many therapists who understand how difficult that would be.

The "letter" Jane wrote for me states that I suffer from a condition called Gender Identity Syndrome, and that in a professional's opinion, hormone replacement therapy and gender conforming surgeries are the correct treatments. Believe it or not, this letter is like the Holy Grail or Willy Wonka's Golden Ticket. I was extremely fortunate to get it quickly so I could be on my way. I found a doctor in Las Vegas who was willing to take me on as a patient and prescribe testosterone to aid in my transition since few doctors are willing to do this.

But before I started anything, I knew my first step was to tell my family and friends. Jane had me choose one person to tell, to "test out the waters," if you will—that one person whom I knew for a fact would take the news in stride, accept me in any form, and would be a big fan of my journey. So you're probably thinking, which one of my parents, or was it my sister, did I tell? None of the above. And the reason being, it felt too risky. My family is and always has been my rock, but my biggest fear was losing that rock, that foundation. Even though we had a new family friend who was transgender and we all loved dearly, she had transitioned many decades earlier so I think it was easier for them to accept her since they had never known her before her transition. I wasn't convinced that having an immediate family member who was transgender wouldn't be too much for them. My family had taken my coming out as gay with grace, but this felt different. I would no longer be the girl whom my parents had given birth to, no longer a daughter or sister. I would abandon my birth-given name, and I would look and sound completely different, and my family would have to adapt to all this. What if I had exhausted all of their patience and understanding over the years and this news was the last straw? And because I was raised in a Christian household, what if they believed the crap others said—that I was turning my back on God and believing He made a mistake. It would've sucked to try out this news and lose my family at the same time, so I decided to make it easier on myself.

I thought about all the people in my life. For those of you I know who are reading this, please know that my not choosing you to be my first was a difficult decision—one I'm sure I made far more complicated than need be, but I was afraid. So the winner was my dear friend Kri. We hadn't been friends for all that long, but during the short time we had known each other, boy did we go through some stuff. Naturally, that stuff all had to do with supporting one another through bad relationships and break-ups, but without them, we never would have been friends. Kri has this dynamic personality that makes you want to be around her. She has a true passion for life and an amazing knack for finding the positive in anything. I have no idea how she does that, but it's a gift. She grabs life by the horns, and whenever I see the quote by Marvis Leyrer, "Life's journey is not to arrive at the grave safely, in a well preserved body, but rather to skid in sideways, totally worn out, shouting holy shit, what a ride!" I totally think of her. I admire and envy her sense of adventure and willingness to try just about anything. This type of friend was someone I knew would be my biggest fan no matter what, and that's exactly what happened.

Kri and I went out for coffee one afternoon, and we sat there and chatted for quite a while as I stalled. We were actually going to go to a meet and greet for a state Congresswoman that was organized by my therapist Jane, and many trans people would be in attendance. I had to tell Kri before we got to that shindig because I was afraid that Jane might introduce me to others in the trans community as Jeremy. Not that she wanted to intentionally "out" me, but more as wanting to use my chosen name and gender pronouns as a way to support my transition. So I got up enough nerve to stutter and say, "Hey, I have something big I want to share with you." Honestly, I have no idea what I actually said or how I got it all out, but I must've done okay because Kri's face lit up. She literally smiled ear to ear and said her familiar phrase, "Yeah!" Her reaction couldn't have been any better. I felt a huge sense of relief, and I was proud of myself. The only thing I do remember from that afternoon was a couple of hours later at the meet and greet, she looked over at me and said, "Oh, you're not gay anymore," like she'd been thinking about that one for a while. I just smiled and said, "Yup."

Halloween was just after that, and I usually went to Kri's aunt's house for her annual Halloween party, which was epic by the way. Every year, I wore male costumes, but this year was going to be better because it wasn't going to be just a costume anymore. I knew Kri would pass along the news to her family, and I was just happy I didn't have to do it myself. So when I got there, her entire family simply swallowed me up with love and support. And to this day, I consider them my second family.

I knew I needed to tell my parents and my sister now; all I prayed for was that they wouldn't leave me. I'm sure when they read this, they will say, "How could you ever doubt we would accept you?" And possibly, it may even hurt them to know I was so afraid to tell them, but fear is a horrible thing, and it perpetuated all of the terrible what-ifs. As a practicing worrier, it's pretty easy to get myself worked up, so even the slightest possibility of losing my family was terrifying.

I told my sister first, and I'll never forget that day for as long as I live. Jayna and my niece Sidney came over to my house to hang out, or so they thought, but I had an agenda. Since Sidney was only about two at the time, I figured it was okay to have this conversation in front of her since she would be clueless, but I underestimated her. Jayna and I were no strangers to having deep and meaningful conversations, but I doubt she thought it would take this turn. Of course, it took me quite a while to get this out, but she was patient. I finally managed to tell her that for my entire life, I had felt out of place, nothing fit, and that I knew inside I was a boy, so I was going to be making some huge changes so that the inside matched the outside. By this time, I was sobbing, and I have to say her reaction was priceless. She laughed. Even as I write this, I'm laughing. Of course, I wasn't laughing at the time, and I was stunned and a bit pissed off at her reaction, at first. Here I was in the midst of an ugly cry and spilling my guts, and she was laughing. She quickly started explaining that she wasn't laughing at me and added, "It's about time! I've been wondering when you would figure this out." She was actually surprised that I thought she would be shocked, and she said that the only one who was shocked was me. Then I laughed too. By now, we were both crying and hugging each other, and Sidney crawled in the chair with us. It was a beautiful moment.

Once I got myself together, Jayna told me that she had a confession to make. She said that Sidney had always thought I was a boy and had been confused when anyone corrected her…until now. She was emphatic that everyone had it wrong and I was a boy. She was and still is an amazingly intuitive kid, far more than anyone gives her credit for. This was a child who used to look up from playing and yell, "Phone!" a few seconds before it actually rang. A bit creepy, but cool, and somehow, she had always seen me for who I really was deep down.

Jayna and I talked and talked and reminisced about all the times growing up that were indicators or red flags to that day's news making sense. We recalled all the times strangers had called me a boy, how I had freaked out about wearing white shirts because someone could see my bra, and on and on. By now, we were laughing, and I began to realize that I hadn't hidden my secret very well from those who really knew me. To say that I was relieved is a huge understatement; I was ecstatic. My last hurdle was telling my parents. I knew that once my immediate family accepted me, I would be able to widen the circle and tell others, but first some baby steps.

I'm not sure whether I really thought my parents would disown me, or by now, it was just the worried frenzy and fear that had clouded my judgment, but I was literally nauseous at the thought of making a phone call to them. At this time, my parents had moved from Las Vegas to Hawaii to fulfill their lifelong dream, so I couldn't just pop over to their house to drop this bomb on them.

Seeing my fear, Jayna offered to give them a call for me, and of course, I jumped at the chance to chicken out. So the plan was that she would head home to make the call, I would stay home, soil myself, take a nap, and wait. I never realized how letting go of the biggest secret of your life could be so exhausting. Thankfully, I didn't soil myself, but I was able to take a nap and sleep.

Later, Jayna called and said she had had a great conversation with our parents; they loved me, supported me, and would call me that night. The only detail she shared was that at first they weren't home so she left a message, saying it was very important to call her back ASAP; she told them I was fine, but she needed to tell them some really big and important news. I guess when they called her back, their main concern was that I was okay and safe, which seems natural since I had put them through some scary years. When Jayna told them the news that I was transgender, she said she could hear my dad in the background asking, "What is it? What is the news?" And she could tell my mom took the phone away from her ear, and loud enough that my sister could hear, she said, "Everything's fine; it's what we've talked about." Holy Shit. So if anyone reading this book was expecting a sad story of rejection or persecution, this isn't that book. And yes, I know how incredibly blessed I am, and I will never forget it.

Apparently, my parents had discussed the possibility of me being transgender many times over the years; in fact, my mom told my sister that she knew the day I was born. Now that would've been good information to have about thirty-eight years earlier, but then again, I never would've had the opportunity to take the scenic route to manhood. My mom has never really explained what she meant by knowing since the day I was born, and I haven't asked because it doesn't matter. If they had a reason why they knew, but never shared with me, then I accept that. My parents did an amazing job in raising me, and I don't need to know anything more than that.

So while I was waiting for my parents to call me that evening, my sister thought it would be a good idea for me to go out to eat with her and her family to keep me busy. And I just have to say that from that night on, my brother-in-law Jay has been amazing and has treated me like the brother that I am, and in fact, he has taught me a ton about being a great man, and I know I can ask him anything.

So we were in the midst of getting ice cream when my cell phone rang…. It was my mom. Anyone trans or not, gay or straight, can attest that hearing your mom's voice say, "Hello" and "I love you" makes you know it's going to be okay. The moment was priceless, and I didn't care who saw me cry. The tears came easily and I embraced them. Even though my mom immediately said the things I needed to hear, my heart was still pounding so hard that I could actually see it through my shirt, and I knew I was shaking, though I'm not sure why. It felt so freeing that my core family was so happy for me, and we all became closer that day. And even better, my mom, through her tears, said to me, "I just need to give you a hug; we need to see you in person and let you know how much we love you," and they booked me a flight to go out to see them.

Within a week, I was in Hawaii with my parents. I felt such overwhelming love from them. I felt like I was finally authentic and not hiding, and I'm sure it was refreshing and possibly scary for them to experience me this way. Over the next few days, we talked, laughed, and cried. They asked questions and I answered every single one of them. I guaranteed them that they would be more embarrassed to ask than I was in answering. And one word of advice for anyone going through this same situation—it's natural for people to have questions, and not all of the questions will come out right, but the fact that they're asking means the dialogue is open. We discussed what changes lay ahead for me physically and emotionally, and the big question for them was, "What is your name going to be?"

My sister and I had already had this discussion, and we knew that, had I been born a boy, my name would have been John after both of my grandfathers, as well as, my dad's middle name. But now I already had a cousin named John, and honestly, that name didn't fit me. My family is big on everyone's first name starting with the letter J, and I wanted to keep with that tradition. When I came up with the idea of Jeremy, my sister lit up and said she was thinking the exact same thing, so that was that. I like the name a lot, and also, if someone slipped and called me "Jenny," it would be easy to blow it off. When I said "Jeremy" out loud, I liked how it sounded. Up until that moment, I had always hated my name, and I typically mumbled it, so what's funny is that so many times on the phone, people thought I said "Johnny." Ironic. Another cool thing about the name Jeremy is it's very similar to my dad's name, Jerry. I didn't want to be a junior, but this was close enough and a way to be like my dad. So since my dad was somewhat represented in my name, I wanted to keep my middle name Lyn as a connection to my mom and sister. They have the same middle name too, which is actually my great-grandfather's first name. The entire name just feels right, and I'm proud to tell anyone—no more mumbling.

Now that I had complete love and support from my immediate family, the next task was to cast the net a bit wider. So I wrote a letter to those closest to me whom I felt needed to know about my new journey. It wasn't a long list—a few close friends and extended family members, all of whom were out of state. I must've written, rewritten, modified, and edited that bad boy 100 times until I was finally comfortable enough with the short and sweet letter. The letter wasn't anything fancy, but it definitely got the point across. Oddly enough, writing it wasn't as nerve-wracking as dropping the letters into the mailbox. Once they went in that box, there was no turning back, and I'm pretty sure it's a federal offense to crawl in one of those blue mailboxes and take stuff out. And I'm definitely not prison material. So off they went.

The next week was excruciatingly long as I waited to see whether anybody would respond. And then it happened; I had two phone calls from very dear friends of mine, Jen and Gerald. Thanks to caller ID, I knew it was them, but I didn't answer. Here is my public apology to both of them: I know it took guts for you to make those calls, but I was scared and, oddly enough, embarrassed. This was a very raw, confusing time for me, so I punked out. They were calling out of love for me and I blew it, and for that, I am truly sorry and remorseful. Both of them left amazingly beautiful messages of how proud they were of me, thrilled for my future, and how thankful they were that I told them. So often in my life, I didn't believe people liked me, loved me, or wanted my friendship, but in those calls, I believed them. And to this day, we have continued amazing friendships even though our busy lives and many miles keep us apart.

Every single person who received that letter has been supportive, and not only are they still in my life, but our relationships are better and stronger, I believe because I finally opened up and let them in. I received well wishes in cards and emails, and it felt wonderful to share myself genuinely for the first time.

I received an amazing letter from my Aunt Judy that touched me deeply; if you recall, she is the one who saved Christmas by getting me the "boy's clothes." The gist of the handwritten letter was that even though my news came as a bit of a surprise, she and my uncle supported and loved me the same. Growing up, we lived two houses down from my aunt, uncle, and cousins, so they were in my life from the get-go and knew me very well—the good, the bad, and the ugly. I don't think I hid my struggles very well, so living so closely together, I'm sure they saw everything.

After the responses I got back from my letter, I was truly humbled to know how much I was loved and I meant to others. I had wasted so much time making incorrect assumptions and making myself lonely. But I now had an opportunity to make up for lost time.

CHAPTER 4

LET'S GET THIS PARTY STARTED

*"Your life does not get better by chance,
it gets better by change."*

— Jim Rohn

Now that the hurdle of telling others, and myself, was over, now what? Saying I'm transgender is one thing, but now came the real work. Where to begin?

My transformation began with my boobs. Ha ha. I had always hated them and they were a constant reminder of the wrong body, so naturally, they were a good place to start. No matter how I dressed or stood in front of the mirror, there they were. Mine weren't large, but they were big enough, and the fact that they were even there on my chest just pissed me off. So not knowing exactly how to start, I found a website that sold trans-related stuff like binders and packers, or to be blunt, boob smashers and prosthetic dicks. But first the binder. A binder is exactly what it sounds like; fabric, or the like, that basically binds or squishes down your breasts, making them appear flat and like a man's chest. This can be done in many different ways from wrapping an ace bandage tightly around the chest or buying actual binders, but either way, they are uncomfortable. I tried the ace bandage route, but I could never get it right, so I found this website and thought it had the answer.

On the website, these binders looked like sleeveless athletic shirts in different colors. The models wearing the shirts were thin and very athletic-looking dudes, and my desire to look like them overshadowed practicality and reason. The description said something to the fact that for trans guys, these compression shirts were comfortable and would smooth out your chest to look more masculine. Fantastic! Well, with a description like that, who wouldn't want one? I was sold; sign me up for two because I would be living in those suckers. Did I mention that I'm gullible? Anyway, each compression shirt was about $35, but in my mind, it was money well worth it, so I ordered one in white and one in black. And then I waited.

When the doorbell rang about seven to ten business days later, I knew what was at the door—a new me! Anyone who has or is wearing a binder knows that's not true. Since I had tracked the shipment online, I stayed home from work that day so I would be there when they arrived. I literally ran to the door and there was the box on the porch. I quickly opened the box and tore open the plastic bag covering each binder, then ran upstairs to my bathroom to give it a try.

I was so damn excited, and sensing this excitement, my dogs ran upstairs with me. They were excited too, yet they had no idea why.

Off came my shirt, and there I stood in front of the mirror shirtless, thinking, "As soon as I put this binder on, I will look like a man." As I tried to pull it on over my head, I quickly realized that the compression fabric didn't have a lot of give to it, but I guess that makes sense if it's really going to smash things down. So I tugged and pulled. Now I had it over my head, and one arm was stuck up in it, trying to peek out of the sleeve hole. Hmmm, I looked at the torn plastic bag that I had tossed on my bathroom floor, hoping to see some directions, but there were none. Now I was starting to sweat a bit, and my right arm was actually stuck in the body of the shirt with my right hand poking out through the neck hole, my hand almost resting on my face. I couldn't move it up farther to the armhole, and it wouldn't back out the way it went in. I'm not even sure how I got my hand stuck in the wrong hole. If anyone has ever seen the TV episode of *Friends* when Ross gets stuck in his leather pants, you have a tiny idea of what was going on in my bathroom.

Now I was really sweating, turning pink, and beginning to panic. In the mirror, I could see my fat squishing out from every possible place it could. I was stuck. The body of the binder had rolled up to my mid-back and was now trapping my left arm to my side. I thought for sure this was it; I would suffocate and die. I looked over at my dogs, who were just staring at me, and said out loud,

"Oh no, I need help." They didn't do a damn thing.

I was completely panicking, and the only thing I could think to do was somehow to get in the top drawer of the bathroom vanity and find some scissors. I managed to get the scissors out of the drawer after many tries, and I turned them around enough to make a few cuts around the neck hole, without slashing my own throat. The few cuts were not enough, so I ended up cutting through the entire thing, splitting that bad boy right down the middle. The relief of being able to breathe again was like in cartoons when a character is too full of air and someone puts a pin in him; then all the air comes out in a fart noise and he flies around the room. Yeah, it was kind of like that, except the only noise was me saying, "Fuck."

I was so pissed, even though I had circulation back in my extremities and could take in a full breath again. What the hell? Why didn't they come with directions? I could've been killed! Okay, I don't think I've ever heard of death by binder, but there's always a first time. Once I calmed down a little, I realized that the models on the website were flat-chested, fit, cis (non-trans) guys. They didn't have to cram anything into the shirts and probably wore a larger size so they could get them on with ease for the camera. What had I been thinking? That afternoon, I went from pure excitement to absolute despair in a matter of fifteen panicked minutes. My idea of having a life-changing experience had never factored in common sense. Boy, do I hate when I do that.

Needless to say, that was my last binder experience, and both went into the trash that day. In hindsight, I should have returned the second one or at least given it to someone else, but the combination of anger, embarrassment, and fear of someone finding out what I was doing was why it ended up in the trash. If I'd already thrown away multiple, brand new books, why not this, right? So for now, I would continue to wear dark colors and shirts a few sizes too big so I could hide. I just needed to figure out a way to get rid of my boobs permanently.

Boy, am I glad my bathroom can't talk. Crazy shit has taken place in there. Besides experimenting with binders or drawing facial hair on my face, the next thing I decided to try was a packer that I could use to stand up to urinate, commonly referred to as an STP or "Stand to Pee" device. I had bought different sized packers just to stuff in my underwear, but I hated wearing them, and they always felt uncomfortable. Probably because, like most guys, I bought a much larger size than was necessary, so it always looked like I was some perv walking around with a boner. Not a good look. Some packers are designed just so you can have a bulge of various sizes; others can be used for sex, and then STPs allow you to pee without having to sit down. For trans guys, standing up to pee is something many of us think about, wish for, dream of, and now thanks to STPs, can actually do. When I was really young, like six or seven, I remember trying to stand up to pee, which didn't work well unless I was straddling the toilet backwards. I don't recommend it, nor would the person who has to clean the floor.

So there I was again on a website looking at pictures and descriptions of various STPs. Much like the binder, I was at the mercy of these Internet photos and reviews, so I wasn't really sure what I was getting, but they sounded awesome. I mean, after the binder "situation," things had to be better, right? So when I ordered my STP packer, which was far more expensive than a regular packer, I decided to be realistic and go for the small. Once I chose the size, I picked the color closest to my skin tone, but it still looked fake. This particular STP, from Peacock Products, had a built-in funnel that easily caught and directed urine out of the rubber shaft. Easy enough, and even the photos and online video made it look simple and stupid proof.... Again, I'm in.

Peacock isn't an American company, so it took almost a month to get it, but true to form, I tracked it online every step of its way. I waited impatiently, but the big day finally came. Naturally, when it arrived, I didn't have the urge to urinate, but I stuffed it in my underwear, downed a bottle of water, and waited. And then for good measure, I decided I should drink another bottle of water. I wanted to make sure the maiden pee would be epic. In fact, once I had the urge to go, I held it, making sure my bladder was full. Now, I do have to mention that this product did come with instructions, but urination instructions...please. I got this.

Finally, it was time. I built this moment up, as I do, and I had envisioned, from here on out, rolling up to a public urinal, whipping out my rubber dick, and peeing like a racehorse. Since I was just hanging at home, my STP was snuggled in my tighty whities, and I was wearing my sweatpants and socks. I went upstairs to my bathroom, pulled my sweats down to just above my knees, and managed to get the dick through the flap in the underwear. I held the funnel part tight against myself, which was just behind the balls, and with the other hand, I held the rubber wiener and aimed for the toilet. I'm pretty sure I was smiling. Here goes nothing. I relaxed and let loose, and some pee came out the tip. Hooray! Then my underwear got real warm and I could feel something running down my legs.

Yep, I was pissing my pants. I looked down and urine was overflowing the funnel and coming out from everyplace possible, except where it should. I had waited too long to go, so I couldn't stop. I stood there in my bathroom, hand on my dick, and completely wet myself, including the floor. Now why didn't I just turn around and sit down? Well, the thought never crossed my mind. The difference with this disastrous experience versus the binder was I didn't get mad. I literally began to laugh, and I laughed some more. Un-fucking believable. I had just peed my pants…priceless. I was so thankful that I hadn't tried this out in public. Once my bladder was empty and my pants and socks were full, I undressed, showered, and did some laundry. And, of course, then I looked at the directions. The very first thing it said was to use the STP in the shower until comfortable and to control the stream of urine so you don't fill up the funnel too fast. Duh! From time to time, I practiced with this STP device at home and pretty much got it down, but I can't seem to bring myself to taking it out into the world. All I can think of is peeing my pants, so for now, I prefer to do that in the privacy of my own home.

I ended up trying out various binders and STPs and revamping my wardrobe—it was extremely liberating to put everything girly or perceived as girly into a garbage bag and drop it off at Goodwill. I kept a few things that were borderline because even though I had started the emotional and mental transition, not much else was changing yet, so I still needed to be able to float between passing as a girl and a boy. I wasn't out to anyone beyond my safe zone. Jayna cut my hair, even though my hair was already short, but sprucing it up into a more traditional man's cut made me feel better. I cleaned out my house and tried to make it manlier, even though I had no idea what that meant. So my next step was to take a real leap of faith and make some permanent changes.

Since I was already in therapy and had my Golden Ticket letter, I just needed to find a doctor so I could get on hormones. For whatever reason, most primary doctors won't do testosterone injections for an FTM (Female to Male); however, some doctors are okay with giving you refills, but not the initial prescription. That one doesn't make sense to me. So by doing Internet searches, talking to other trans people, or getting referrals from therapists, eventually a doctor can be found. I was fortunate that I met a trans woman in a support group, who referred me to her doctor in Las Vegas, who had a large trans patient clientele. FYI, be prepared to pay out-of-pocket because many insurance companies won't help or will make you fight for reimbursement. Because this doctor knew that, he didn't overinflate the cost of office visits, and he tried his best to steer everyone to more affordable pharmacies to get their hormone prescriptions.

So I made the appointment and was excited, yet nervous for my first visit. My sister, being the trooper that she is, went with me for moral support. When we got to the doctor's office, no one was in the waiting room, which helped my nerves because I had envisioned a packed waiting room where everyone would know why I was there and would stare at me with judgment. Yes, I know how irrational that thought was, but it was a real fear for me. As I filled out the paperwork, it really hit me that this was it; no longer was I going to talk about changing—I was going to make it happen. I was taking action. Once I was in the exam room, the doctor came in. He was very nice and welcoming. He told me all about testosterone, how to inject it, and how I would be monitored going forward, as well as some of the effects that would take place. He also detailed somewhat of a timeline for when to expect the changes.

Honestly, I was so nervous that I don't remember what he said, especially when he was giving me the directions on self-injection. I watched a few YouTube videos once I got home, so I was caught up for the most part. He administered the first shot during my appointment, which really stung, probably because I couldn't relax my butt. Testosterone is thicker than water, so the needle had to be a bit bigger, as in girth, not length, and coupled with not being relaxed, I developed a huge bruise a few days later, which, of course, I showed to everyone at my weekly support group because I was proud of it.

I know it sounds crazy, and I'm sure it's just a placebo effect, but I felt different after that first shot. Psychologically, I felt better, like I was in control of my life for the first time. I was really making this happen. My first shot was on November 18, 2008, and within a month of that shot, I was in San Francisco, undergoing a full mastectomy. I know all of this sounds extremely fast, but you have to remember that I had been thinking about and mentally planning this for a very long time. Anyone who has the chance to speed up this process would take it.

I had been doing research online for many months, looking at the different doctors who specialized in FTM breast removal surgery, commonly referred to as top surgery. I narrowed it down to a few and then decided on Dr. Michael Brownstein in San Francisco because of the results I saw online; plus, a guy in my group had gone to him a few years earlier and was extremely happy with his choice. Every time I called Dr. Brownstein's office, the staff was so nice and helpful, but what really sold me was when I called one time, Dr. Brownstein actually answered the phone and addressed all of my questions as if he had all the time in the world to listen to me. I was lucky enough to get an appointment with him very quickly, and without thinking the finances through, I took it.

As you can imagine, major surgery like a full mastectomy with chest reconstruction isn't cheap. (I'll discuss the financing of such surgeries later in the book.) And even though I had health insurance at the time, this was definitely not covered. I must say, though, that Dr. Brownstein's costs were not astronomical because he knew most patients were paying out-of-pocket. He really understood that he was not only changing lives through his surgery, but also saving them. The one awkward part was since I didn't live near his office, I had to email photos of my chest for our consultation. I guess it was better than paying for a flight and hotel just for him to check out my boobs, but nevertheless, I was extremely uncomfortable taking the pictures and then sending them off. That's definitely one selfie that will never be on Facebook.

My goal was to have this surgery before the effects of testosterone therapy really kicked in. In my head, I envisioned testosterone turning me into this burly, hairy guy, and I wanted to make sure that when that happened, my boobs weren't staring back at me in the mirror. Again, I am truly blessed that I could make so many changes all at once because for many trans guys, this is not an option, due to money, timing, or support. So with my surgery scheduled for December 10, 2008, I mailed off my $500 deposit to hold my spot and had this unbelievable faith that somehow I'd make this work out.

I now had a couple of months to find the money. My sister was on board with this plan and said she would be happy to go with me to San Francisco for my surgery. I started the paperwork at two different banks for a small loan, as well as for Care Credit, whose website describes it as "payment options for health-care expenses," which was exactly what I needed the loan for, so I gave it a shot.

Around this same time, I flew out to see my parents in Hawaii. After our initial discussions around the whole transgender revelation that I mentioned in the last chapter, they also wanted to know what my plans were in regards to making physical changes. I told them of my immediate plans of being on testosterone shots and that I had made an appointment with a surgeon to have my breasts removed. I also told them that someday I planned on having surgery to reconstruct my genitalia, or at the very least, have anything female removed, but that wasn't important at that moment. I filled them in on how I was going to pay for the surgery and how I had it all worked out, assuming I got the loan. That was pretty much the end of that discussion, and I have to say they took all of this really well. A lot of information was dumped on them, and either they were dumbfounded, or they finally realized that my life was changing for the better right in front of their eyes.

The next couple of days were spent enjoying each other's company, laughing, reminiscing, and having honest conversations. Not once did I ask them for a dime. They had bailed me out financially one too many times, which I am eternally grateful for, but I didn't want to ask for help once again. But what happened the morning I was to head home stunned me. Sitting out on their lanai, having coffee and chatting, my dad casually brought up the topic of my top surgery again. He said that he and my mom had been discussing it, and he then handed me a check, which was made out to me for the full amount of my surgery. He followed up by saying, that as my parents, they had watched me struggle from such an early age, always trying to fit in, to find myself, to stay alive, and of all of the things they had paid for in my life, like my college education, nothing seemed as important as paying for this surgery. He said they were literally contributing to my wellbeing and happy future.

Even as I write this now, I have tears, so you can imagine there was not a dry eye in their house that morning. Part of me didn't want to take the money because I felt guilty that once again my parents were bailing me out, but the way they offered it, I knew that wasn't the case. I humbly accepted their gracious and beautiful gift. Again, I know my experience with my parents may not match the experience of many transgender people with their own parents, and maybe I haven't had the same struggles, but each of us is only familiar with our own lives and stories. I am blown away with the blessings I have been given.

Now that the obstacle of money for surgery was gone, especially since I was turned down for a loan, I focused on therapy and getting ready for my life to really change. I continued with my shots every other week, and I decided to have a goodbye party for my boobs—a boob-voyage! Naturally, a small, very select crew was invited, and it was fun. This was probably the first, and most certainly the last, time I gave those puppies any attention.

As I said, things moved quickly, and before I knew it, my sister and I were off to San Francisco. The day we arrived was my pre-op appointment and my first time meeting Dr. Brownstein in person. He went over all the logistics like where and when to be in the morning, what to do and what not to do the night before, what the procedure entailed, and basically what I could expect over the next ten days. He was great, and I felt even better about choosing him as my surgeon; I mean how can you go wrong with a doctor who brings in his dachshund Frank to work with him every day? Frank, who has since passed away, was a very cool office mascot, and I know he put many at ease.

The next morning was the big day. Jayna and I took a cab from our hotel to the surgery center, and boy, was it early. I filled out the last bit of paperwork, changed into my snazzy surgical gown and cap, and waited for the anesthesiologist and doctor to come in. Many people have asked me whether I was nervous, but I can honestly say, "Absolutely not." I had slept really well the night before, and I woke up calm, with my only thought being, "As long as I wake up after surgery without boobs, all is well in the world. And if something were to happen during surgery and I don't make it, my last few hours on earth, I will have been completely happy."

An IV was started, and Dr. Brownstein came in and drew on my chest with a sharpie, making notations for himself. He had me stand up to do this; it was a bit awkward standing topless in front of a doctor, a nurse, and my sister, but I knew that experience would never happen again, so I just kept my eye on the prize. I was standing because, as women know, once you lie down, your boobs tend to run for your armpits. And then it was time to go. I hugged Jayna tightly, told her I loved her, and walked with the nurse down the hall to the surgical suite, climbed up on the table, and the last thing I remember, I was chatting about my various tattoos. Good night.

I've heard that you tend to come out of anesthesia still thinking about the last thing on your mind before you went under; at least, that was true for me. One of the last things I said to Jayna was, "Make sure you get a picture of me as soon as I'm in recovery." I wanted to document everything. Once I gained enough consciousness to remember, I opened my eyes, saw Jayna, smiled, and asked her, "Can you take my picture?" She and the two recovery nurses began laughing. Apparently, this was about the tenth time I had "awakened" and asked that exact same question. Guess this was very important to me. Not only did she get my picture, but she took a video of it too; yet another thing that will not be on Facebook. Once I really came to, enough to sit up and talk, I was discharged and went back to the hotel. It still amazes me that a serious surgery such as a mastectomy is done on an outpatient basis.

I was so drugged up that when we arrived at the hotel, I stopped and got in line at the little coffee and doughnut kiosk. Jayna vetoed that. After a little nap, I got out the San Francisco city maps that I had collected the day before and told Jayna that tomorrow we should get up and hit the cable cars because there was so much to see and do in the city. Yep, I was still high as a kite. She just responded with, "Sounds good, but let's see how you feel in the morning."

The next morning when I woke up, I realized why she had said that. I could barely move and felt like I had been run over by that cable car. Chest reconstruction surgery is kind of major, and I guess I didn't really think about the recovery process. I was only focused on the breast removal. I was bandaged up so tightly and had a type of binder over the top of the bandages, so I couldn't see my new chest, but I could see the drain tubes coming out from below the bandages. Every few hours, we had to empty the fluid that collected into these clear football-shaped things at the end of the drain tubes. I guess this was to make sure that fluid didn't build up under the skin. To keep the tubes and little footballs from flapping around, they had been safety-pinned to the sides of the binder. I remember, distinctly, the nurse going through the drain-emptying procedure with my sister and me, putting a lot of emphasis on "Do *not* pin these to your pants." I didn't fully understand why she was making a big deal out of this until the first time I went to the bathroom. She had heard of others making that mistake, and when they went to pull their pants down to go to the bathroom or get undressed, they had yanked the tubes out of the skin. Ouch!

For the first few days, I had to have help doing almost everything, from getting in or out of bed and getting dressed to, unfortunately, pulling down or pulling up my pants to go to the bathroom. Thankfully, I had someone with me whom I knew very well because it was embarrassing enough. Jayna was amazing and took such great care of me; however, she drew the line at wiping my ass. I think that's fair. I never realized how much I used my arms in a day until I had to keep them by my sides. Just trying to put on a button-up shirt was painful enough.

Each day I felt a little bit better and stronger, and we were finally able to walk next door to the IHOP for a few meals. Eventually, I could make it a block or two around Fisherman's Wharf, but I never lasted long. With the drains in, I was a bit hunched over, and with every movement, I could feel them tug at the skin, which was a creepy sensation.

By the second week, I was able to get the drains removed. When I went into Dr. Brownstein's office to get them taken out, I'm not sure what I thought he was going to do, but just yanking them out was not it. However, that's exactly what happened. By now, scabs had begun to form around the tubes coming out of the sides of my chest. As I lay on the exam table, Dr. Brownstein cleaned up the scabs, told me to take a deep breath, and exhale fully. So I took a full deep breath, and as I began to exhale, he pulled. It was quick, and with a smile, he said that didn't hurt him a bit. At least he had a good sense of humor at just the right time. When he showed me the tubing, which was about 8-10 inches long, I knew why I was so hunched over and uncomfortable; there was a lot of tubing under the skin. He put a Band-Aid over each hole, and when I got up, I instantly felt better and was able to take in a deep breath.

I only had a few more days in San Francisco until I could have the stitches around my nipples removed and then head home. During the surgery, my nipples were removed and cut down to a smaller size and then sewn back on in the correct position. So the only stitches that were visible and had to be removed were around my nipples; the other stitches below my breasts were dissolvable and covered by tape. So on our last day in San Francisco, we checked out of the hotel and headed back to the doctor's office for my final visit and stitches removal. The area was and still is numb so I didn't feel a thing. It was at this visit that I finally saw my new chest, and to be honest, it looked like the nipples were in the wrong spot. I later consulted my brother-in-law, and he assured me they were fine.

And just like that, we were back in the cab, heading to the airport to go home. The only small snag with this entire trip was that our flight was canceled due to snow in Las Vegas. Are you kidding me? I've heard that, "Every time a bell rings, an angel gets its wings," but apparently, every time Jeremy gets his boobs cut off, Hell freezes over.

Looking back, the recovery process was pretty quick. I had to wear a binder, which was basically a medical tube top, that Velcroed on, for about two weeks at home, and I had to keep the nipple area cleaned and covered with gauze. The surgical tape covering the large half-moon incisions on my chest eventually wore off. Each day, I felt better than the day before, and it was weird, yet very cool, to see myself in the mirror. I definitely looked rough, but my chest was flat. Slowly, but surely, the scars started to heal and became less pink. Applying scar ointment daily was the key. I'm beyond happy with the results, and I feel like Dr. Brownstein gave me a new life. Within six months, I was sitting in my backyard with my shirt off. It felt so strange, like I was so exposed, but I forced myself to do it.

Before long, I left my house and the security of having my own private backyard and moved into an apartment. I forced myself to go to the community pool a few times a week and to sit out with my shirt off, just to get over my anxiety. The scars were really healing up and their placement made it look like I actually had pec muscles, unless you were up close. I was extremely uncomfortable, but not one person stared or said anything. I was a nervous wreck, so I only went during the day when kids were in school and most people were at work, but the point is, I did it. Slowly, I was living the life I had dreamt of, and who I've always been on the inside was finally visible on the outside. Having a tan also made me feel better.

It's now been six years since I had top surgery, and I still don't have any feeling around the scars except for the occasional nerve itch, which is just annoying, and every once in a great while, I can still "feel" my boobs, almost like phantom breasts, but I no longer look down to see whether they're still there. In the beginning, that phantom sensation happened so often that I would look down to make sure nothing was there or I would rub my chest for reassurance. At times, I would have dreams that I would wake up and my breasts had grown back. Thankfully, I don't have that nightmare anymore. I guess it's true that time does heal.

A few years ago, I decided to get a tattoo over the scars as a way to boost my self-image. I already had numerous tattoos on my arms and various other places, so to tattoo my chest wasn't a stretch. I found a great place in Las Vegas that specializes in Polynesian tribal work, and when I went in for the consultation, the artist didn't even flinch when I took off my shirt and told him what I was looking for. The guy literally drew a design on my chest with a ballpoint pen; I checked it out in the mirror, and it was exactly what I was looking for. Thankfully, most of my chest was numb; otherwise, those next four hours would have been a bitch. Only a few spots near my armpits had feeling, but the rest was good to go, and anyone who has had ink done on a ribcage or sternum tells me I am damn lucky I was numb. I was told that a lot of artists won't tattoo over scar tissue, but this guy either knew he was helping me have a better life or he didn't care. I'd like to believe it was the first, but either way, I was getting it done. Once the tattoo was finished, I stood up, somehow kept my composure, and didn't cry because, just like magic, my scars had disappeared. Having this tattoo has given me such a boost of confidence that I can walk around shirtless, hang out at the beach or pool, work in my yard, you name it, and I know that people are checking out the tattoo, not my scars.

So after having top surgery and being on testosterone for about two months, I knew I had to start telling people that I interacted with on a semi-regular basis, especially through work, about the change I was undergoing. Things were happening quickly so people were going to figure this out. I couldn't hide forever, and I wasn't moving away anytime soon. Like I mentioned before, my family and I owned our own business, so I knew I wouldn't lose my job. Many other trans folks don't have that same security, and coming out at work can have negative consequences. Losing your income is a reality for some transgender people.

In my business, we were the franchisor for a major haircare franchise and had about ten franchisees, or independent business owners, below us. I remember my dad saying to me, "If one of our franchisees doesn't like it or can't handle this news, they can leave; we don't need them." Now, that's not entirely true, but I appreciate the sentiment. At first, I only told the owners of the ad agency we worked with, and one of our radio advertising reps, both of whom had become personal friends. They all took the news like champs and were amazing. I knew they would handle this news in stride, but they exceeded my expectations. All three of them were thrilled for me and were honored that I shared my story with them; their only concern was that I was healthy and happy. And from that day forward, any time I saw them, I was addressed as Jeremy and referred to as he or him. I instantly had built a fan base.

For a few months, these friends were the only ones at work who knew about my transition. The last time my franchisees had seen me was about two weeks after top surgery when we'd had our year-end meeting, and unfortunately, before the meeting started, a franchisee came up to hug me like she usually did, and I reactively stopped her because I was sore. When I put my hand up to fend off the hug, she looked shocked, so I said, "I'm sorry; I just had some minor surgery," without thinking. Now that I had brought attention to myself, it was noticeable that I was now flat-chested. I didn't have the guts to tell her or anyone else the truth because I was too scared and not ready to come out as transgender.

By the end of the day, a rumor had spread around the room that I had had a mastectomy because of breast cancer. I don't know exactly how that happened except someone had privately asked my sister whether I had cancer, and she said something to the effect of "Not that we know of; as of today, she's healthy." I feel terrible that Jayna was put on the spot like that, and we should have talked this through before the meeting, but neither of us knew what to do. So it was inferred that either my surgery was preventative care or the mastectomy took care of any disease I was battling. I didn't realize this rumor was taking place until after everyone had left and my sister mentioned it. To be honest, because I didn't know what to do or say, I didn't correct anyone and I just carried on as if nothing had happened. It just became something we didn't talk about. I have always felt extremely guilty and remorseful about this misunderstanding, and I'm truly sorry for my actions or lack thereof. For the next six or seven months, I stayed away from being seen by any of my franchisees and did all my business through email. No one thought anything of it and just gave me my space, and Jayna stepped up and took on the entire role as the face of our company. But hiding and deceiving was definitely taking a toll, so I couldn't let this go on any further, nor was it fair to put others in a position to keep my secret. Now that I was starting to look and sound like a male, I had to disclose my transition.

Because of the incorrect story that was floating around, I felt I needed to protect Jayna so she was not perceived as a liar or would be opened up to ridicule or blame. I was afraid others would lash out at her and demand to know why she didn't tell them the truth, so I wrote a letter to each of them, explaining what was really going on. I started it with saying that I was presented with an opportunity to change my life, and that my life was never in danger from a disease but from my own hand. I apologized for keeping them in the dark for so long and hoped that we could build better working relationships going forward. I don't know whether the people I did business with will ever read this book, but if they do, my deepest apologies for deceiving or perpetuating a deception. Please know that it only came out of absolute fear.

After I mailed this letter to each of my franchisees at their homes, the reactions I got were incredibly positive. I received email responses as well as a few phone calls, and some business relationships did get better. Sharing myself in a more authentic, honest, and humble way made it possible for others to get to know me. One franchisee, specifically, one that we seemed to struggle with for common ground, called me and told me that he was absolutely thrilled for me and that he personally guaranteed he and his family wholeheartedly supported my transition. It was an incredible moment, and from that day, I feel it healed our working relationship.

Even though how I got the information out to people wasn't the way I had wished for, once I came out as transgender, I felt free. It is true; the truth shall set you free. And while it's not comfortable by any means to transition "out loud" and at work, I have been so fortunate and blessed to be surrounded by a growing network of support.

CHAPTER 5

LOOK OUT, A HURRICANE IS COMING

"Patience is not the ability to wait. Waiting is a fact of life. Patience is the ability to keep a good attitude while waiting."

— Joyce Meyers

By now, I had been on testosterone shots for about seven months, had healed up from top surgery pretty well, and was finally noticing some minor changes. Of course, I had grand expectations of being a full-blown man with a thick beard and mustache after a couple of shots, but the transition didn't work that way. I guess I had forgotten that puberty the first time around didn't happen overnight, so why would it now? I remember my therapist saying to me, "Enjoy the early stages of transition, take each experience in, and absorb it because you will never get those moments back." When I heard that advice, I thought she was full of shit. I was thirty-eight years old; I didn't have time to take this in; I was in a hurry, or more accurately, I was completely impatient. And no, I didn't marinate in the experience; in fact, I was downright pissed that it was taking so long.

I felt like the awkward phase between being a girl and actually passing as a man took forever, and this in between stage was embarrassing and physically painful. Each and every day when I woke up, I went to the mirror, looking for any signs of change. Mostly, I noticed my face and body getting really puffy, and the texture of my skin, mostly my face, began to change and felt and appeared rougher. And even though I was gaining weight, the fat was starting to move away from my hips and settle toward the front, giving me the appearance of a big beer belly. None of my clothes fit, and my joints ached all the time. And when I say ache, I mean the joints of my hands and feet literally throbbed 24/7. Between the weight gain and the physical pain, I began to wonder whether it would ever get better. Not to mention that my mood swings were violent, and I could no longer keep my emotions and anger in check. It literally felt like I was spinning out of control, and I didn't know what to do about it. I didn't want to tell anyone how I was feeling because I was so afraid that someone might say, "Are you sure you made the right choice?" There was no question in my mind that I was doing the right thing, but I was in a vulnerable place and wouldn't have been able to handle anyone questioning my journey.

It got to the point, in terms of my anger and moods, that my own family was afraid to talk to me. So again I withdrew and became a hermit, making a tough situation even harder on myself by trying to go it alone. Testosterone was changing me physically, mentally, and emotionally in ways I wasn't ready for—I was going through puberty again, but this time, in a matter of months. That's a lot of change going on. With my hormones really kicking in, I began to struggle to keep myself together. I had been under the impression that once I started my transition, everything would be better, but the truth is I wasn't handling it well, and I wasn't patient with myself. My emotions were completely out of control, and I didn't know when or what would set me off. I would be fine one minute, and the very next, "Holy shit! Look out! Hurricane Jeremy is coming!" much like I was in early adolescence. I did a splendid job of continually pissing off my family, and I'm amazed that they stuck around.

It didn't help my rocky emotions when some of the transition changes would come and go unexpectedly, like my crackling voice. When I was ready and expecting change, it didn't come, and when I wasn't prepared, there the changes were, causing me to be on edge. I remember one of the first times that my voice cracked; I had been around my house most of the day, and apparently, I hadn't spoken to anyone yet, so when the phone rang, I answered only to hear a strange squawk come out of my mouth. I was shocked, embarrassed, and excited. For those of you who are old enough to remember the episode of *The Brady Bunch* where Peter's voice started to change…exactly. At times, my voice was the same; other times, it sounded like I was getting laryngitis, and then sometimes, it just squeaked, but the only thing that I could count on was the unpredictability of it. When the phone would ring, before answering, I would literally say, "Check, check, hello" a few times, feel good about the deep, strong, and confident sound of my voice, and pick up the phone. Then out would pop a high-pitched and squeaky "Hello." Dammit. This scenario happened many times when my dad called. He would ask whether I was getting a cold, and I would snap back at him in anger because I thought he didn't get it, and I was embarrassed once again to tell him my voice was changing. That would set me off and I would cut the conversation short.

I was so frustrated with everything, and I hated going through puberty in middle age and in front of others. Even though I was excited for some of these very early changes, I didn't want any attention brought to them. I just wanted everyone around me to pretend almost that it wasn't happening; however, I never conveyed that and was upset that they couldn't read my mind.

I later found out that my hormone levels were way off, but before knowing that, I slid back into a depression. I had really hoped that my days of depression were behind me because what should I be depressed about? I was becoming who I was meant to be. Like I said before, there was no question in my mind that I am transgender, but I was starting to wonder whether I was really strong enough to go through it. Maybe depression was a coping mechanism, a comfortable, predictable place to hide in. I was familiar with depression, and oddly, it provided a bit of security during a very unstable time. Going back to living as a female was out of the question, and if I didn't think I could pull off transitioning into a man, what were my options?

By now, I had let my temper get the best of me, and I had my first and only experience of punching a wall. Man was that stupid. I don't even remember what I was angry about, but this rage swelled up in me, and I felt like I just needed an outlet, so the wall took the brunt of it. The wall didn't even move, and the only thing that I got out of that was a swollen and bruised hand. I really don't recommend that. Honestly, I was starting to scare myself, and I couldn't imagine living my life like that.

So one day when I didn't think I could take anymore or had the strength to be a man, I found myself cleaning my house from top to bottom. I got my pertinent papers out of my safe and laid them out on the kitchen counter. I made the decision that this was the day I was going to give up. Even though I had made it this far, I doubted my strength and courage to complete my journey. I had a few errands to run for work, but when I returned home, my plan was to take my ID out of my wallet and place it on the kitchen counter, get my dogs in the car with me inside the garage, turn the car on, and wait for death. I didn't want to leave a mess, and

I wanted to make sure that I could be identified, so that's why I cleaned my house and left my papers visible on the counter. I also didn't want to abandon my dogs, and because I wasn't thinking clearly, I thought they would be better off in the car with me. I wasn't rational anymore, and I felt like I was just going through the motions of living, like I was numb.

When I returned home that afternoon, I went to the mailbox like I did most days, and in it was a letter from the county telling me my house was scheduled to be auctioned off, since I was in the foreclosure process. For the last six months, I had been working with my lender to come up with a way to keep my house from going into foreclosure, but I hadn't fought that hard, and I was actually looking forward to getting out from under that debt. Even though I knew this outcome was coming, I hadn't expected it this soon. The auction date on the letter was only two weeks away, and this notice was to advise me to vacate the property.

As I stood in my living room reading this letter a couple of times, I literally dropped to my knees, sobbing. Not because I was losing my house. I looked straight up in the air and said out loud, "I get it." Without a shadow of a doubt, I heard the voice of God say to me, "Not today, not ever, and for now, I'm going to take your garage away from you." I felt His presence and His arms around me as I cried, and for the first time in my life, I knew I would never harm myself, or even entertain the notion of taking my own life.

Thankfully, as I have mentioned before, I had grown up in a Christian home and my faith was strong. There are those who may think that being transgender goes against Christian beliefs, so how could someone who is transgender be a devout Christian? Well, I will only speak for myself, but I can tell you that God has been with me every step of my life and has always known my path. God doesn't make mistakes; therefore, I am not a mistake, and He believes I am strong enough to live this life and make this transition. And in that moment, I truly knew how much He loved me, that I was not alone, and that everything was going to get better.

And just like that, things did get better. I picked myself up off the floor, wiped the tears from my face, and put my papers back in the safe. I stuffed my ID back in my wallet and called my sister. I never told her all the details of what happened that day, but skipped to the part about losing my house. She said she knew of a great apartment complex that was being built nearby and that she would go with me to check it out. I had this amazing calmness about me, and within the hour, she and I were looking at the apartments. I signed a lease and made an appointment with a moving company. Not many people feel that losing your home to foreclosure is wonderful, but in my case, it was one of the best days of my life. That day I began to live fully, and I was so grateful that God had spared my life. He has big plans for me; I'm supposed to value life, help others, and share my story.

Within two weeks, I had moved into my new apartment and started to settle in to a new life. Little by little, my voice began to settle down, and as I exercised more and watched what I ate, my body started to change as well. The weight came off faster than it had ever before, and I was finally feeling better about myself. A few hairs started to show up on my face, even though I was the only one who could see them. I had started shaving after my first month on hormones, but it wasn't until now that there were actually a couple of hairs to shave off. Eventually, a very light and patchy beard would present itself, and I was coloring it just so someone could see the hairs. I was really hoping for a Grizzly Adams beard, but that was not in my future.

With just a few subtle body changes and the deepening of my voice, I was starting to pass as a guy more often. It was awesome and awkward at the same time; when people called me "Sir" or referred to me as "he" or "him," etc., it sounded strange at first, but each time, it boosted my confidence. Unfortunately, I would have some days where no matter what I was wearing or doing, I would get called "Ma'am" or "she," and I felt deflated when that happened, mostly because I was embarrassed. I didn't always correct people, and I often pretended that I didn't hear it. Most of the time it happened on the phone, so I would just gloss over it and think of a ton of things I should've said after I'd hung up. And again, because I am impatient, I wondered whether I would always have a girly voice. Not that I have a deep Wolfman Jack type voice now, but it's definitely deeper than it was, and it fits me perfectly.

Some of the most awkward times were when I had to pay for something with my debit or credit card because I hadn't changed my name and gender marker on my license or cards yet. So as I started passing as a man more and more, I still had my old ID, which confused a lot of people. I probably could've changed that a lot earlier, but I wanted to pass fully as a man first. I've had other trans guys ask me, "When is the right time to change your name, gender, etc.?" but I don't know what the right answer is, except I would say, "Do what feels right to you." So I would be out shopping and all would be well until the dreaded moment of having to pay. I typically tried to pay with cash, but sometimes that didn't work out. My anxiety would build as I approached the counter to pay and prayed that it was a machine where I swiped the card myself, or the employee would be careless and wouldn't check the name of the card or ask for ID. But as luck would have it, most of the time, I encountered the employee of the month who did everything by the book. So when that happened, I would hold my license or card with my thumb over the first name; that typically worked, but naturally, there were times when the cashiers would take the card out of my hand to scrutinize it, then look at me, look back at the card, and look back at me with confused looks on their faces. My reaction was just to smile and shrug. Whether they got it or not, they were nervous and just handed me back my stuff and said, "Thank you." I'm sure it's just my imagination, but I always thought the worst and assumed they were judging me.

I knew I was getting more comfortable in my skin when I went to vote one day. The presidential election was upon us, and I'd never missed a chance to vote since I had turned eighteen, so I wasn't about to now. I knew voting might not be as easy as I wanted it to be because I now looked like a boy, but I still had a female license and voter's registration card in my old name. So I called the voter's registration department and explained the situation; fortunately, the woman on the other end of the phone was awesome. She said, "Definitely go and vote, and if you have any trouble while you're there, have the voting center give me a call," and she gave me her direct line. Now that's customer service. It felt good to have some backup, but I was really nervous.

When I got to the polling center, which was in the elementary school by my house, there wasn't a big crowd; in fact, I could probably count the number of voters on one hand. All of the volunteers working that day were seniors, not as in high school seniors, but more like Wal-Mart greeter elderly…oh, crap. I walked up to the table and handed them my voter's registration card like it was no big deal. Within seconds, not one, not two, but three workers were discussing my registration card and looking at me. No offense to senior citizens, but they can't whisper. So now the entire polling place was involved. Perfect. I calmly said, "Is there a problem? And if so, please call so-and-so; she's expecting your call." Well, they didn't know what the hell to do or what to say. There was one poor high school girl working there as well, who looked at me with a smile as if to say, "I'm so sorry," like she understood my situation but didn't know how to make it any better. And then the one little old lady holding my card said to me in her loud whisper, "So, I guess your parents wanted a girl?" Clearly, she didn't get it and thought my parents had named their son, Jennifer. Seriously? I just leaned in and said, "They used to have one" and smiled. At that, the high school girl was laughing and so was I. In the end, I got what I wanted, which was to vote. Can you just imagine the conversations that took place after I left? Priceless.

As with most things, patience is the key. I created so much anxiety because I couldn't be present in the moment and appreciate the changes, good or bad. I always wanted more changes, faster or different changes, and I had taken on an all-or-nothing mentality. While I feared judgment from others, I failed to see that I was judging myself harshly and that I came at most situations ready for confrontation, well before it happened, if at all. I struggled with giving myself any credit for being courageous enough to begin this journey and almost gave up too soon. During the early stages of transition, it was easy to get caught up and be consumed with searching for changes or having unrealistic expectations. Looking back, I wish I had been able to relax more and appreciate the process. As they say, hindsight is 20/20, and if I could now, I would have done things differently and treated people better, especially myself, but I have to believe that rough patch was integral to becoming a better man.

CHAPTER 6

PUBERTY 2.0

"The secret of change is to focus all of your energy, not on fighting the old, but building the new."

— Socrates

Ah, puberty—it was so awesome the first time around, why not do it again at thirty-eight? Without a doubt, puberty can be a horrific, embarrassing, and downright awkward time in anyone's life, but at least in your teens, everyone around you in school is going through the same hot mess, so you don't stand out as badly. But doing this in your late thirties, not so much. So in addition to the mood swings and voice changes I talked about in the last chapter, let's now add in acne, hair growth and loss, and a sex drive that went through the roof. So anytime I had wished I could do things over, I should've been more specific because puberty wasn't it.

Let's start with the acne. I was very fortunate my first time going through puberty that my acne was, for the most part, manageable and wasn't all over my face. Of course, at the time, I thought it was horrendous, and it was one more thing that I added to the list of things I hated about myself. Over the years, I would go through times when my skin completely cleared up and then times when it would break out, mostly on my chest and back. But for the most part, I thought the days of battling acne were behind me, but oh, joy, they came back with a vengeance.

My skin didn't really start to flare up until I had been on testosterone shots for about seven or eight months, and then it just took off. I've heard other trans guys say that it clears up over the years, but we've already established that I don't have a lot of patience, and coupled with my anxiety, no wonder it would break out. I feel like I tried every over-the-counter medication or gimmick out there; most would work for a very short time and then stop, so it seemed like I was wasting my money and stuck in a vicious cycle. I even tried taking antibiotics to get it under control, but that bothered my stomach, and neither my doctor nor I thought it best to be on them long-term. It wasn't until my fifth year into my transition that my acne began to calm down and became far less noticeable.

Just within the last year, I switched from testosterone injections every other week, to a testosterone implant, which consists of small testosterone pellets implanted under the skin of my hip/butt area. The pellets gradually dissolve over five to six months and keep the hormone levels nice and even. The up-and-down fluctuations I had while doing self-injection played havoc on my moods, as well as my testosterone and estrogen levels, so it made sense to give the implant a try. Of course, not having to inject myself with a needle was a huge plus. I was definitely a hesitant shot giver and dreaded doing it, so it always hurt and left a bruise. I never got to a place where I was able just to prep the area on my butt and quickly stab the needle in; rather, I would get the area all cleaned up and think too much and hesitate, which meant I didn't push hard enough, so you could see the skin indent under the needle until the needle finally made its way through the skin, all while my hand was shaking. I think it's safe to say becoming a phlebotomist is not in my future.

One time I was in my bathroom performing this painful ritual, and as I was deep in thought and really concentrating on the shot, something set my dogs off and they started barking furiously, which in turn startled me so badly that I flinched. When my hand jerked, the needle was only halfway in, but I managed to ram the two-inch needle all the way in and yank it out, within a fraction of a second. Blood started to pour down my leg, and I was frantically dancing around the bathroom, trying to find something to stop the bleeding. I grabbed a towel on the rack and managed to stop the hemorrhage. I was visibly shaking, mostly due to anger. I got myself cleaned up and had to redo the entire shot because I never got the juice in me, dammit. Thank God there was never a video camera in my bathroom.

From that day on, when I was ready to inject myself with the needle, I would start to distract my dogs by having a full on conversation with them. I guess I was thinking that if they were concentrating on listening to me, they wouldn't hear anything outside to bark at. Not the most sound logic, and in hindsight, I should have just put them outside and shut the door, but instead, week after week, my dogs and I discussed life. I'm now into my second dose of pellets and so far so good. My hormone levels are much more consistent, and I believe this is the reason my skin is starting to calm down. Hooray!

Another bodily change that came along with T-based puberty was hair loss and gain. Of course, you lose it in the places you want it, and you gain it in those that you don't. Such is life. Hair loss is probably the only side effect that I don't want, so I constantly check my head for any signs of a bald patch. My forehead seems to be growing, but fortunately, that's the only noticeable hair loss so far. I've heard that you can get a glimpse into your own hair loss by looking at the males on your mother's side of the family; if that wives tale has any truth to it, I should be okay. While the guys on my mom's side have all seemed to retain their hair pretty well, they can't grow a beard worth shit, which should have been my first clue, but I have one uncle who can, and of course, he's the one I hone in on.

I knew I would get a bit hairier, but I wasn't expecting to grow hair on my ass. That doesn't seem necessary, but what are you going to do, right? I started to get a few stray hairs on my chest, nothing noticeable, and none of my body hair has a specific pattern, except for the cool little "happy trail" of hair that starts below my belly button and creeps down below the waistband of my boxers. The hair on my legs and arms is much thicker and coarser, but I'm stoked that my hair color is light enough that I don't look like a baby bear. None of the guys on either side of my family are hairy, so I don't expect to be the exception.

Speaking of growth, this second puberty phase was where my libido really kicked in. Not to say that I didn't have one before, but it definitely wasn't as pronounced. I now know why teenage boys take so long in the shower and why they shower often. At first, it was cool because I felt young and vibrant, but over time, I have to say it was annoying. To be blunt, getting myself off was more like a chore that had to be completed before I could think or do anything productive. I was definitely too old for this. If I ever mentioned this to anyone who knew I was trans, the next question was always, "Is it true that you get bigger?" No one ever said what "it" was, but they usually pointed to their pants. Obviously, I knew what they were talking about, and to flat-out answer that question, yes. For those of you who don't know what I'm talking about, let's catch you up. For trans guys, one of the best side effects/changes that takes place with testosterone therapy is the clitoris gets larger. Of course, we all want it to keep growing to a full-size penis, but that never happens. So how big does it get? Well, that's different for every guy, and it can range from about one to three inches, with increased girth as well. Let's just say I'm average. There are surgeries to gain more size and be able to stand to pee, but I'll get into that later.

So if you add up an increased sex drive and the beginnings of a teeny weenie, it equated to a newfound interest in Internet porn. To be honest, up until this point, I hadn't checked out porn on the Internet, and I wasn't interested in *Playboy* or similar magazines. The only experience I had with checking out porn was watching the scrambled X-rated channels on cable as a kid, and that was just to see whether I could see something. I never did. So how it started was, I was just curious about how cis guys had sex with women. Most guys will tell you that looking at porn is just what guys do; it's no big deal, but unfortunately, my curiosity eventually gave way to an obsession or, more accurately, an addiction. I would spend hours searching for a video in which either the guy resembled me or the woman looked like someone I found attractive.

It may sound crazy, but because I couldn't have sex with a woman in the same way that a guy with a full functioning penis did, I used these videos as a way to live vicariously. I didn't grow up hearing the normal raunchy locker room banter or overblown sex stories that guys tell each other, so I felt like I was the odd man out. I was trying to make up for lost time. By no means was I looking at porn as an indicator on how to treat women or even what they liked in bed because pornography is the worst place to find that, and if you ask me, the women in porn look miserable and are treated like crap. My addiction to watching was more of a wishing or longing for (no pun intended) the sexual intimacy or experience that a cis guy could provide and I couldn't. And before long, I couldn't break free from this obsession. Because of the embarrassing nature and shame of porn addiction, I had a difficult time asking for help. I shared my struggle with a few guys in a church group, but I left out my backstory and transition. I wasn't completely honest, so eventually, I found myself lying and telling them I was doing the work and getting better. It wasn't until I saw a counselor at church that I finally addressed my addiction and started to make progress on dealing with my issues. There were times when I felt so out of control and wished I had never been curious in the first place.

As I said before, we can all agree that puberty is awful. That's a given, but for someone who is transgender, it feels like the end of the world. In our teens, our bodies betray us and almost solidify that we are morphing into the wrong body, the wrong gender. Non-transgender kids may look forward to the changes as their bodies mature, such as boys getting facial hair, muscles, and basically becoming men. Girls develop breasts, curves, and turn into lovely ladies. But when I was growing up, going through puberty was like a death sentence. I wanted the facial hair, the muscles—anything that would let the world know I was becoming a man.

Because before puberty, I could almost forget that I was a girl. I could play "boy" sports, wear "boy" clothes, and hang out with the guys since little kids all kind of looked and acted the same anyway. Everything's different after puberty.

In Puberty 2.0, the changes happen pretty quickly, and when I look back, it's now hard to envision who I used to be or how I looked. Seeing old pictures of myself is like looking at photographs of someone I recognize but don't know. The old life seems to slip further and further away with time, which feels amazing. And the photos taken during mid-transition make it seem laughable that I even thought I passed as a guy during that time. I don't care who you are or when you went through puberty, the pictures will document that you looked like a dork, and I'm lucky enough to have two sets. In the midst of this puberty, I was completely embarrassed and hated having to go through it in front of what felt like the entire world. There were many times when I thought I would be stuck in this limbo forever and never be taken seriously as a man.

Fortunately, limbo was only a year or two. The physical changes happened more quickly than the emotional and mental changes, and as I mentioned earlier, hormones brought out my inner beast. Just as it sucks to be around any other teenager, I was no different. Once I emerged from puberty and calmed down, I allowed more people in, or maybe they just weren't as afraid to be around me; either way, I became more social. It was then that I was able to reach out to some of my guy friends and ask them to share their puberty experiences, mostly to check whether what I was going through was normal—whatever normal is. They all agreed that I did it right; it sucked for them as well, but at least this time around, I was legally able to drink.

I'm thankful to have a good group of guys around me as a sounding board so I was able to ask them all kinds of crazy questions without judgment and too much embarrassment. It was like taking a Becoming a Man 101 crash course. They made sure I knew the key basics like don't chitchat in the men's bathroom, keep your head down, and don't even look like you're catching a peek of someone's junk. I was actually surprised to find out how self-conscious guys really are since I thought it was just me. By observation and hanging out with these guys, they caught me up on how guys walk, shake hands, talk to each other, which is typically about nothing important, or share an embellished story—just the typical day in the life of the average Joe. This was probably the first time that these guys had to articulate what it means to be a man, and I hope we all learned something from these lessons. I mastered when to use a handshake, a fist bump, or the bro shoulder bump/hug. That last one is quite popular, but use it carefully. Toss out a few "What's up, bro?," "boss," "champ," or "dude," and you've had yourself a full conversation.

Because I had more of a boy's experience as a child and had always known I was male, none of this information seemed new, but I appreciated the refresher course. I already walked like a guy and always hated spending any time in the women's bathroom, so I had always known to keep my head down and skip the chitchat. I was also a fan of not sharing too much of myself, so maybe I wasn't as behind the eight ball as I had thought. The best part about hanging out with a group of guys is that nobody asks you what you're thinking or how you feel! Like I said, most times, it's just light banter, rehashing sports, or boasting about things everyone knows is untrue, and it's awesome.

As my physical body and mental and emotional states really started to come together—better than they ever had in my whole life—I began to notice my confidence was really starting to take hold and showing up in the way I carried myself and interacted with others. As the world was beginning to see me as a man, I began to stand taller. Most of the time, I came across as very confident, but inside was a different story. I was still my worst critic, and I noticed all of my shortcomings. I guess you just fake it until you make it.

I started working out at home, mostly because I was intimidated to go to the gym, and I'm the kind of person who needs to look like a pro on day one…. Can you say perfectionist? I didn't have a lot of experience with the equipment at the gym and didn't want to look like a fool, so I bought various exercise DVDs and worked out in isolation. That did the trick for a while, but for someone who is already lonely, it wasn't the most beneficial. It wasn't until I moved back to Colorado in 2012 that I decided it was time to go back to the gym. I had been isolated long enough, and because I have a lazy streak, I knew I would need to pay someone to keep me accountable. Even before I started transition, I always had this vision of what I wanted my body to look like, and being hit or miss with exercise and trying to go it alone wasn't going to cut it.

After transition, I refused to become that little fat guy. So last year I signed up with a personal trainer at the gym; he could show me what to do and keep me focused on myself, and I didn't have to worry that others were watching and judging me. By the way, no one gives a crap what you're doing at the gym; everyone is too focused on himself and how he looks. So since I was paying for this, I got over the urge to stay home pretty quickly and found that I enjoyed getting out of the house. The workouts were extremely tough; in fact, I almost fainted in the locker room after my first session. Talk about awkward to have a naked guy grab your arm just before you hit the tile floor. Over time, my trainer pushed me to limits I didn't know I had, and I could finally start to see glimpses of the body I dreamed of. He kept saying, "Just stick with it and give it your best and you will get the results you want."

It took about six weeks for me to start to notice some real changes in my body, but that was all I needed before I was hooked. My pants weren't as tight, I could do a couple of pull-ups even if I had to rest in between, and I was starting to see the outline of actual muscles. Most importantly, I could make it through an entire hour-long workout without wanting to vomit. I was learning so much and gaining the confidence to work out on my own at the gym that I've stuck with it. I am absolutely amazed by my body's transformation and what I am now capable of doing. I've gone from struggling to do one pull-up to doing circuit exercises that include multiple pull-ups, push-ups, and jumps. The first time I ever did multiple pull-ups in a row, I was stunned and grinning from ear to ear. I still have a long way to go before I achieve the look I want, but I'm happy with my progress and now walk into the gym with confidence and welcome the stares. All of the worry about what others thought was such a waste of time and kept me away.

I remember during my first puberty, I struggled with my balance. I'm not sure why because it wasn't like I grew a lot during that phase, but I've heard others have had similar experiences. Maybe because my body was changing and growing in all directions, my equilibrium couldn't keep up; who knows? And puberty the second time around was no different. You would have thought after all those years on the ice, figure skating and playing hockey, that my balance would have been much better, but boy, it was not. I can see why Grace was never my middle name, and it's a wonder that I've never been hurt seriously. Working out definitely helped with my balance and coordination and maybe those things were so off because of my trying to hide myself. I was now trying to navigate the world in a new body and gender, but also in a body that I liked, for the first time. I wasn't used to that feeling.

Before transition, I always felt like I wanted to disappear into the woodwork, especially when my body started to develop into the wrong gender, but, typically, that backfired. If only I had been more surefooted and agile, maybe some of my embarrassing and attention-grabbing tumbles would have been avoided. There's nothing like wanting to blend in and never draw attention to myself, yet if I just trip or stub my toe, all that gets thrown out the window.

In middle school, I managed to draw the attention of an entire gymnasium and accompany it with sound effects. We had a band concert where the fifth through eighth grade bands played and entertained a roomful of parents. I was in the seventh grade and played percussion. After a crowd-pleasing evening, it was customary for all the kids to take the chairs, music stands, and instruments back to the band room. Obviously, being in percussion, our instruments were much larger than most, and due to my very short stature, I had a hard time schlepping the drums and whatnot. So I grabbed the snare drum and its stand because it was more manageable, or so I thought. For me, common sense seems to reside in hindsight. Why I didn't take the drum off the stand and carry them separately, I don't know, but I picked them up together, with one hand on the snare drum head and the other on the base of the stand.

Because I'm short, when I picked them up, the snare drum was at eyeball level, so I couldn't see a thing in front of me. I peered around the side of the drum and thought I had a clear path to the gymnasium door, but unknown to me, the conductor's podium, which is a flat wooden box about 4'x4' in diameter and roughly 1' high, had not been picked up yet and was directly in my path. I ran directly into that sucker and fell smack dab onto it. Not only did I fall onto the podium in front of the crowd, but I managed to break the drumhead when my elbow went through it. I'm sure you can imagine the ruckus I made.

It felt like I was on the ground for a lifetime, but my parents said it looked like it took me longer to fall than it did to pop back up. Once I was back on my feet, I grabbed the drum in one hand, and novel idea, the stand in the other and shot out of the gymnasium like a bat out of hell. Maybe nobody saw that? Who the hell was I kidding? I'm from a small town, so probably one third of the population was sitting in that gym; of course, they saw it. Naturally, I was embarrassed, mortified, and afraid the band teacher was going to make me pay for the broken drum. Once she stopped laughing and saw that only my ego was injured, she assured me that I didn't have to pay for it. I think she knew the ribbing I was going to get later was payment enough.

I had to come back to the gymnasium to meet my parents so we could leave, and by the time I had made it down the really long hallway and caught a glimpse of my parents and sister, it was apparent that yes, indeed, everyone had caught my little tap dance performance. My sister was laughing so hard that she was crying, and my parents were doing their best to keep it together, but they failed miserably. Now as I write this, I'm hysterically laughing, but in that moment, I wanted to die. No one was ever supposed to notice me, but now I had set myself up not only to be noticed, but also teased and ridiculed. Fan-fucking-tastic! I begged my mom to let me stay home from school the next day, but that was a no go. Unfortunately, the teasing was horrendous, but I did survive.

I wish I could say that was the only experience that I've had like that, but as I said, my middle name is not Grace. I could only stay hidden and unnoticed for so long before all that pent-up anxiety would come flailing out. I truly believe my desire to be invisible and keep myself so tightly wrapped inward has affected my balance, coordination, and twitchiness. Working out, on its own, won't change any of this, but being comfortable in my own skin, being okay with being visible, and being able to laugh at myself puts me in a much better place for when something stupid happens in the future. And continuing with my balance-building exercises will hopefully keep me on my feet. Even though going through puberty as an adult was unpleasant, at least this time I emerged as a man.

CHAPTER 7

BEHIND EVERY GREAT MAN IS A GREAT WOMAN

"Grief is not a disorder or sign of weakness. It is an emotional, physical and spiritual necessity, the price you pay for love. The only cure for grief is to grieve."

— Earl Grollman

For as long as I can remember, an underlying and constant theme in my life was a strong and powerful self-hatred. I hated everything about myself, from my name and my appearance to the sound of my voice, my size and physical attributes, and on and on. I was always my own worst critic, but it went much deeper than that. While plenty of people nitpick and are judgmental of themselves, I loathed myself. I was great at telling other people that they shouldn't be so harsh on themselves, all while being a hypocrite. I spent a lot of time in front of the mirror dissecting myself, being disgusted by every little thing. Not that perfection is even attainable, but I clearly thought I was far from just being okay. I thought my nose was too pointy and would always try to flatten it down, my teeth were too big, I was too short, and I felt disproportionate. If only I could change these things, then maybe I would like me, and maybe others would like me too.

I never saw the good things that I had to offer—my kind nature, sense of humor, and a passion for helping others. No, I only saw faults. These flaws gave way to a sense of longing to be someone else. As I mentioned earlier, I would draw a mustache or beard on my face or stand certain ways with my arms folded to cover up my chest and just stare at myself in the mirror. I thought if I could just magically turn into a man, I would like myself so much better; the pieces would fit. Prior to transitioning, all I remember was always being in a state of searching, hoping and wishing for a better life, a better me, and I would be crushed whenever I thought it might not be attainable. I didn't spend a lot of time in the present moment, and rarely was I grateful for the gifts, blessings, and talents that I actually had. My mind and judgment were too clouded with self-loathing to see what was right in front of me.

My self-loathing was probably the reason why I thought I didn't have any friends and that no one liked me. I was projecting my crap onto others, and my head was so far up my own ass that I was blind. When, in fact, much later in life, I learned that I did have many friends and people who cared deeply for me. They tried to be my friends and never really left, even with my constant pushing away of them. Apparently, I was easy to read, and those around me knew I was miserable so they didn't take it too personally. Some left, not because they didn't like me, but because they valued themselves enough not to put up with my depressive self-hatred, and they could no longer watch or support that.

Once I realized I could make some drastic changes to my life and transform into the man I knew I was, I thought everything would change in a flash. I would love myself and I would have more friends than I knew what to do with. So naïve. While the physical part of this process is not long in many aspects, transitioning my thinking and core beliefs about myself have taken longer than expected and are still evolving. And as I have wrestled with this journey, one emotion that I wasn't prepared for at all was grief. Why would I feel a sense of loss? Why the hell would I grieve the loss of a person I hated with every ounce of my being? I've learned that there isn't one particular answer and it's more of a conglomerate of experiences and emotions. I had thirty-eight years of experiences as a woman; whether I liked it or not, that was my story. It was the only life I knew, and even though I believed I was a man, I was raised as a female. All of my life interactions, lessons, and experiences were through a female lens. It may not have always been how I saw myself, but it was what the world saw and reacted to. Everyone saw me as female and just acted accordingly, as we all do when we meet men or women. Why would I be treated as anything else, especially when I never said anything?

So as I was finally being seen by the world as male, I now felt alone and lost. I no longer had any emotional, mental, physical, or social cues that were inherent from birth. I soon realized that the awkward stage of puberty had nothing on this feeling. Think of it this way—each of us learns how to navigate our surroundings and life from an early age according to our gender. Little boys are taught, whether consciously or subconsciously, to be a bit tougher, shake it off, and not to take things as seriously; basically, don't act like a girl. Little girls are reared to be softer, more reserved, and emotional. We see this every day in marketing and advertising, and just from the things that we all say and do without noticing. So when transitioning from one gender to another, it takes much longer to adjust to the mental and emotional changes. When I was in my late teens, I was taught to walk to my car with my keys interlaced between my fingers just in case I needed to strike an attacker, never to park near a big van so I wouldn't be abducted or raped, and to be constantly fearful because bad things happen to women, and typically, by a man's hand.

I remember when I was early in transition, but starting to pass as a male on a more consistent basis, I sat down on a bench next to a woman who had her purse next to her, but tucked in close. I didn't sit too close and even smiled as I sat down, but this woman didn't smile back; instead, she tensed up, grabbed her purse quickly, and held it close to her chest, all while sliding away from me farther down the bench. Now sure, there could have been many reasons for that reaction since I didn't know this woman or her story, but her behavior hit me in a profound way. I was perceived as a threat to her, a perpetrator of bad things all because I was a man. In a split second, so many thoughts ran through my mind, from being excited that she saw me as a man, all the way to wanting to reach out to comfort her and apologize for making her uncomfortable. Of course, I did nothing but get up from the bench to put her at ease, while I stewed in my thoughts.

I realize now that men are afforded the privilege of feeling safer in the world. I have a big problem with this situation. What's wrong with us, our society, and the world, that women have to accept this fear as the norm? As a man, I do feel like I'm less of a target for the same types of crimes, but I feel guilty that I'm now seen as the one who would commit them. I'm still hypersensitive to my surroundings and watch my back closely when I walk to my car, and I don't park next to big utility vans (I think I watch too much TV). After decades of navigating my world as a female, those instincts are difficult to change.

As time goes on, it is getting easier to pick up on traditional male societal cues from just observing other guys or flat out asking guys in my life. It's definitely one hell of a learning curve. At least I've learned what kind of guy I don't want to be or act like. But with that said, it's difficult feeling like a fish out of water, and I'm in a constant state of observing male behavior, while trying to make sure I don't ever act too girly. What's funny is that I realized for my first thirty-eight years that I never wanted to act too feminine either. And again, even though I didn't want to be perceived as girly before and definitely not now, there is a sense of loss in the mere letting go of that girl I used to be. I hated her, but there was security or safety because it was all I had and knew. The self-hatred became my story, my identity, far more than my gender. If I no longer hated myself, had become the man I dreamed of becoming, and liked my reflection in the mirror, what should I do with my old story? It doesn't magically disappear, that's for sure. And, unfortunately, some of it spilled over into manhood. Hating myself became a nasty habit, and as with all unhealthy habits, it was tough to kick. But I slip back into those patterns of thinking I'm less than, or not okay, not because I really believe that anymore, but during times of stress, it is familiar. I'm constantly reminding myself that I don't have to be perfect; I just have to be me.

I've come to accept that grief or loss is completely normal; at least, it is for me. This is my process, and I'm not going to compare it to anyone else's. I'm learning to give myself some slack and deal with all the emotions that come up the best I can, and I have to remember that not everything in my past was awful. My first thirty-eight years were the foundation that the rest of my life will be built on. Encompassed in those earlier years were experiences and events that I wouldn't change for anything. At first, I thought I was supposed to leave all that in the past and reinvent myself, almost like the witness protection program, but that is too much work and downright unnecessary. Turns out, as a person, regardless of gender, I was pretty cool and had a lot to offer. I had achieved a lot of goals like a college education and a career in which I owned my own company, and by the grace of God, I have been financially stable. As the cloud of depression and self-destruction faded, I was able to appreciate fully the good times in my past, which I think has contributed to a sense of loss.

Mostly, I felt like I missed out on a large part of my life because of fear, anger, and hatred. I grieved for the moments that I didn't recognize or give enough credit to, and even though I am still alive and well, I grieved for the loss of Jenny's life. She was the outward face to the world for so long, but all I wanted to do was destroy her, and when I finally had the chance to by transitioning, I rushed through it without thanking her and appreciating my past. That may sound strange; honestly, it does to me as well, but whether you like someone or not, over a few decades, you build a bond. She was gone, and what was left was a strong, healthy man who was going to have to learn to navigate the world without the destructive inner dialogue that kept him from letting go or moving on. For the first time, I felt like I was truly on my own and in the present moment. I didn't miss having her around, but I was in new territory, without knowing what to do. I was scared yet excited.

Transitioning is a very personal and introspective journey, and for me, it became all consuming and selfish. What I failed to realize was that my family and friends were grieving a loss as well. My process took center stage over anything else, and I became judgmental to those around me. I was an ass, plain and simple, and no one else could express any of the struggles he or she was going through because I had to compare them to my transition and trump them. I was not listening and wasn't a good friend, son, and especially, brother. While I think being a little selfish is necessary in this process, it doesn't have to be all consuming. There needs to be room for others to express themselves, too, and if I wanted close, supportive family members and friends around me, the very least I could have done was to be one as well. I had had over three decades to prepare mentally for this transition, but those around me, even if my coming out was not a surprise, had very little time to adjust. Somehow, I forced everyone to catch up in a matter of days or weeks, which is just downright stupid. Again, it was all about me.

As I transitioned, those around me transitioned as well, but I forgot the keyword here, which was "transition." The mere definition, according to Webster's dictionary is, "a movement, development, or evolution from one form, stage, or style to another." I denied others the right to a process or evolution of coming to terms with this new me. Even though they afforded me all the time in the world to stumble and stutter through this process, it still amazes me how many people in my life didn't leave because they put up with a ton of shit from me.

My immediate family, of course, took the brunt of this, and I'm most grieved by how I treated my sister. When I say that my sister is my best friend, I don't say that lightly nor gloss over it by calling many friends my best friend. She truly holds that title all alone. Since we were very young, we've had a special bond, and I've always looked up to her, followed her around everywhere, and probably annoyed her to no end. But in all of my memories, she was always right there; she was my mentor, protector, and guardian angel. She always let me tag along with her and her friends, made sure I was always taken care of, and when I was terrified of the dark, she selflessly let me sleep in her room and never complained. From the time I was in middle school, our bedrooms had an adjoining door which my mom said was for safety reasons, so if anything happened like a fire, we could get to one another, but I saw that door as a lifeline that I was never alone. Living out in the middle of twenty acres in rural Michigan, it was dark and creepy. Throw a thunderstorm into that mix and that's the perfect beginning of an ulcer and insomnia for me. Again, without complaint, my sister let me leave the door open, forgoing that coveted privacy that most high school girls demand. All for me. That door was a lifeline that remained open for many years, but when Jayna went off to college in Hawaii, it finally closed. Things were never the same after she left, and I took it really hard and couldn't even go in her room.

The next couple of years were rough for me as I've said before; that was the time when my mom would call the school every day, checking to make sure I had made it and hadn't driven into a tree on the way there or back home. It was also when my sister, who had been thriving so well on her own in Hawaii, left college to move back home. I didn't know until much later—she didn't tell anyone—but the only reason why she left a place she loved was because she loved me more. My whole family was worried that I might actually kill myself, so she came back home to be my lifeline. This must've been an extremely difficult decision for her, one that I am eternally grateful for. She stayed for a semester and kept an eye on me. I had already been in and out of the hospital by that time, and I was feeling better or at least doing a much better job of faking it, so she felt confident enough to head back to Hawaii and her own life. Time after time, Jayna has always supported me whether I knew it, asked for it, earned it, or was grateful for it. Not that my parents didn't do the same, but something about my sister was special. Siblings could easily drift apart and get absorbed in their own lives, but not her. I gave her plenty of reasons to leave because the more angry and depressed I got with my life, the more I lashed out at her. Instead she just delved deeper into a role of the big sister, protector, and mentor.

Unfortunately, I didn't take into account how my transition would affect the many roles she played. Of course, she was still my big sister, but I was no longer the little sister, so she had to adapt quickly to having a little brother. Her role of mentor would change because she couldn't guide me through a second puberty as a male since it was foreign to her as well, so again, she would have to adapt to mentoring me in different ways. Of course, she was happy for me and was thrilled that I too was now happy, but she had lost her sister. What did that mean for her memories? It truly was like a death for her, a death that wasn't okay to talk about, according to me. I wanted to leave my past behind and pretend I was never a girl, as if the first part of my life never happened, but it wasn't just my past; there were others involved too who didn't want to forget it and let it go.

It took time for me to realize that I didn't want to forget that past either. My sister and I have so many great memories that have nothing to do with gender; they are just about being siblings/best friends. It wasn't until Jayna took a huge, courageous risk and wrote me a letter describing what she was going through that she basically put me in my place. The letter was very difficult for me to read, but it was so necessary to jar me from my selfish and nasty stupor. She described in detail her grieving process, which made me take my head out of my ass and get a clearer view. I know she was nervous to send that letter, so when I called her after reading it, all I said was "I'm sorry" and "You're right. I can and will do better." Since then, we have both worked through our grieving processes and are enjoying our new sibling relationship of brother and sister. We both realized her roles haven't really changed; she still helps and advises me when it comes to clothing and hairstyles and protects me like big sisters do.

Now that I'm actually present and listening, I'm learning a lot more from her than I ever did before. She was the one who gave me my first "guys" haircut, and with it came a pep talk about how "dudely" I was. Her role of protector has now changed into being my biggest fan. She showed her support of my transition by going with me to San Francisco for my chest reconstruction surgery. And even though she had a young daughter at home at the time, she made arrangements so she could be with me for those two weeks, without question. Getting away from a four year old for two weeks may have had something to do with her decision, but knowing her, probably not. And she's already volunteered to be by my side whenever I have any additional surgeries. Without a doubt, I know that my sister will always be there for me no matter what, whether I realize I need the help or not, and I will strive to be the best brother I can possibly be to her.

It has been a constant struggle to remember how far I've come, how courageous and empowering this journey has been, and to have daily gratitude. Some days are better than others, but I continue to persevere. Thankfully, now I can actually look at myself in the mirror without picking myself apart, and I can find good qualities about myself and know that I have people in my life who love me because I deserve it. As I'm working through the grieving of thirty-eight years, I can look myself in the eye in a mirror and say, "I love you" and mean it. There is a full-fledged man looking back at me now, and behind my familiar blue eyes, I can finally see and appreciate that all of my past experiences and life lessons were necessary to become the man I am today. I do have a lot to offer this world, and being able to say, "Yes, I have walked a mile in someone else's shoes," offers a great perspective. I'm learning to appreciate knowing both sides, and I feel that starting out as a woman will make me a better man. It's been said that behind every great man is a great woman; I completely agree.

1971 - A few weeks old
Jayna and me

4th of July 1971
My mom, sister & me in matching outfits

3 or 4 months old

1974 - 3 years old. My sister's 1st day of school. Not sure why I was dressed up.

Halloween 1975
My dad, sister, maternal grandpa, and me

Kindergarten 1976

Christmas 1975
My mom and me

Christmas 1977
My dad and me

Ann Arbor Melody on Ice
Ice skating show debut

Christmas Miracle outfit

Loved the outfit so much
I wore it any chance I got

Melody on Ice skating show

Halloween 1981 - 10 yrs old
I loved my lumberjack beard & mustache!

Ann Arbor Amateur Hockey
1982 - pee wee division

My dad and me dressed as chimps in a suit. Loved being just like him.

High School Varsity Men's Hockey
Senior year

Here's the glamour shot!
Wouldn't have been the `80s without one!

My first tattoo – 18 yrs old
Believe it or not, that wasn't a perm!

Me & Jayna - 1990

University of Colorado
Women's Ice Hockey - 1993

University of Colorado
Graduation 1994

1995 - With my dog Jake
Photo by Marianne Martin – Boulder, CO

Post Massage School days
1998

One of the last attempts at being "girly"
2003

Jayna and me - 2006

Summer 2007 – About a year away from beginning my transition

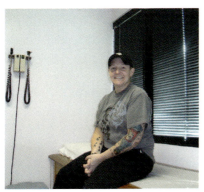

November 2008 - At the doctor's office awaiting my 1st testosterone injection!

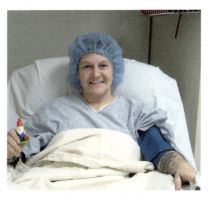

December 2008 "Top" surgery day! I'm ready!

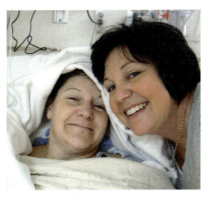

Fresh out of surgery. Barely coherent but smiling!

4 days post-op…doing great!

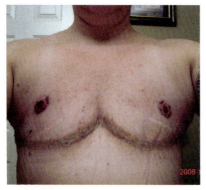

2 weeks post-surgery. Nipples look rough.
The tape is still on the incisions &
my chest broke out from the binder.

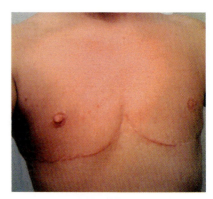

6 months after surgery.
Healing nicely!

Awkward transition period.
I wasn't passing well at all

One year into transition

Making progress…slow & steady
With my dogs 2010

Things are finally coming together. Even have
a bit of facial hair (if you look closely)

My niece Sidney and me.
This is my very first suit!

My dad and me on my 40th Birthday

July 2012 - My family and me
celebrating the sale of our company

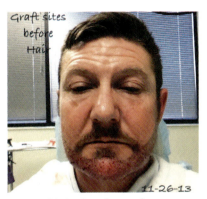

2013 – Beard transplant
Graft sites are ready for the hair!

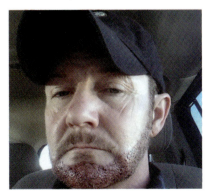

The day after the transplant.
Looking & feeling rough!

9 months later & hair is growing!

2013 – Free to Breathe 5K . I ran in honor of my mom, she's a lung cancer survivor!

My friend Kri and me at my Welcome Back to Vegas surprise party – 2014

2014 – Finally getting some muscles! (And a beard)

Brought back the lumberjack 33 yrs later…with my own beard!

My kids and me
Photo by Fred Morledge – PhotoFM.com

Finally happy!
Photo by Fred Morledge – PhotoFM.com

CHAPTER 8

TO PEE OR NOT TO PEE

"Get comfortable with being uncomfortable."
— Jillian Michaels

Ah, the bathroom! Strange topic for a chapter, huh? For those who are not transgender, your thought may be, "Why is there an entire chapter about the bathroom, and what is he going to share about that?" But for those who are trans, you might be thinking, "Just one chapter?" I don't care who you are; the bathroom is just an unpleasant place. This chapter isn't about all the types of elimination that go on in there, and there's already a book by Taro Gomi titled *Everyone Poops* so that's been covered. But so much more goes on in bathrooms for those of us who are transgender, much of which isn't really talked about, specifically in public restrooms.

If you Google "fear of public restrooms," it's amazing how many articles pop up, but what I'm talking about is different than this fear. Many trans people, myself very much included, have anxiety about using public restrooms, especially early on in transition or if they are not always able to pass as their true gender. Here's where a ton of trans guys are lucky, as we can eventually go stealth, meaning we pass as a biological male 24/7 and basically disappear into the crowd. No one has a clue that we are transgender. It breaks my heart that some trans women are not afforded that luxury, as secondary sex characteristics have taken hold through puberty, such as a larger body frame, lower voice, facial hair, Adam's apple, etc. While many cosmetic or surgical procedures can minimize a lot of that, some simply can't afford them or choose not to partake in those options, so they may not pass as well, to the same degree.

The fear of everyone knowing or getting "outed" seems to ramp up in and around public bathrooms. Bathrooms are an intimate and exposing place, and of course, having a phobia of them is real and valid. Phobias are typically characterized by an irrational fear of something, but unfortunately, fear of restrooms for those who are transgender isn't irrational at all. Some trans people have been threatened, outed, violated, and physically harmed in public bathrooms, and it doesn't take many instances of that to instill a real fear.

Could such an incident happen to me? This is something I have thought about on more than one occasion. If another guy finds out that I'm trans, what would he do? Would he freak out that I'm in the bathroom with him? Would his insecurities be masked with a violent outburst toward me? Would I be banned from going in the men's room? These are legitimate questions and fears, especially since, when coupled with my female upbringing, I still fear men. But having said all that, my personal experiences during transition have been benign at best, and even if I'm out with guys who know my trans status, the bathroom has been okay. For the most part, my anxiety around the bathroom is self-driven, and over time, I've relaxed a little bit more. I still hate public bathrooms, but who really loves them?

During my first few times in a men's bathroom, early in transition, I was extremely uncomfortable. Back when I didn't pass as male all the time, I would pick my battles and sometimes chicken out and use the women's bathroom as a safety net; other times when either I was more confident or up for challenging myself, I would use the men's. But I knew that once I started passing more frequently, I would have to leave the security of the women's room behind. I used to ask my dad and brother-in-law, Jay, over and over, "Are you sure no one will think it's strange I use the stall?" I'm not sure whether either of them gave it much thought, but they both said the same thing, "No one is looking or cares."

In fact, I've come to learn that a lot of guys use the stall because they are uncomfortable using the urinal in public. Guys may joke about it, but there seems to be a genuine concern of someone else catching a peek of their junk. Not the "all confident" gender I thought guys were. That actually makes me feel better. My dad and Jay's advice to me was always, "Just walk in with confidence like that's where you belong, head to the stall, and do what you need to do. But don't forget, no chitchat or pleasantries at the sink. Get in, get out." While that sounded easy enough, for me, as a worrier and over-thinker, it wasn't. I worried about some of the dumbest things while I was in there, "What if the door opens up while I'm on the toilet with my pants down and someone finds out?" or better yet, "What if 'they' know I don't have a dick because I'm sitting down, and it sounds different when a woman pees versus a guy. For guys with a penis, it's much louder because the urine is traveling farther to the toilet when you're standing. It's like the difference between a garden hose being on low with a soft sprinkle versus full on power washing, or at least it is in my head. Did I mention I think too much? So to alleviate this fear, I perfected the "silent pee" or phantom urination.

I must say that over the years, my bladder control is top-notch, mostly from holding it so long to avoid having to use a public restroom at all, but also from being able to control the stream so it makes little to no sound. It may sound crazy, but this is my reality, and it makes me feel better. So if there are other people in the restroom, I initiate my "silent pee," which means I urinate very slowly, controlling the stream so it doesn't make a sound. It's one of my unique talents. And if anyone even gives notice to me being in there at all, which is doubtful, he just assumes I'm sitting in there taking a dump. Give a couple of coughs and a fart, and I'm good to go.

I've gotten so controlled with my stream that I can flush the toilet, pee as hard and as fast as I possibly can while it's flushing loudly, and cut it off mid-stream when the flushing stops. I'm not sure whether this is a good ability to have, but in my head, it's necessary. Of course, I could use an STP device and alleviate a lot of this nonsense, but again, we've established I'm better off to have this worry versus the fear of pissing my pants in public. How I haven't had a urinary tract infection in the last six years is a wonder to me.

I've also noticed that some guys are proud of the size and girth of their poop, so it's always acceptable to drop a load in a public restroom, no questions asked, no judgment or embarrassment, as long as there is a courtesy flush. It's never okay to leave a floater behind, just saying. You're not supposed to save your prize-winning poo for others to marvel at; just flush it and brag to your friends that it was way bigger than it really was. If someone were to ask whether I missed anything from my past life, I can honestly say, the women's bathroom. Not for the primping and gossiping that happens in there, but because it is so much cleaner and smells better. Seriously, how do so many guys miss the toilet and pee on the floor? I'm not the only one who should be sitting down.

A couple of years ago, I went into an Old Navy to do some shopping. I had been in there a while so I'd had to go to the bathroom for some time, but I was holding it to see whether I could wait till I got home. I also knew the bathroom there was really small with only one stall, and I hated that set up. Its awkward having to wait in a small, confined bathroom for the stall to open up, especially when I already have bathroom anxiety. So I finished up and bought my stuff, which the clerk put in one of those large paper shopping bags with handles, the kind that makes noise when you bang it around or bump it with your legs and such. It was inevitable; I had to go so badly that I wouldn't be able to make it home; I would have to go there. So I took my large, noisy bag and headed to the back of the store to the men's room. And when I got in there, it was empty. Glorious! So I thought.

The stall door was ajar and you couldn't see the toilet area since it was a really huge handicap accessible stall and the urinal was in the way. Naturally, when you don't see feet and the door is open, it is safe to assume the stall is empty. As I tapped the stall door open, I heard, "What the fuck?" And out of the corner of my eye, I could see an enormous beast of a man sitting on the toilet. This poor guy had been all hunkered down for a long winter's poo, nestled on his throne with his pants around his ankles, and not a care in the world. How anyone can be that relaxed in a public bathroom is anyone's guess, and maybe he wasn't. For all I know, he could have had the same anxieties and fear of the door lock malfunctioning and popping open, but once he had pulled his pants down and committed to the task at hand, it was too late to get up and close it. In the moment, I didn't think about or care how he felt; I thought only of myself and totally panicked.

TO PEE OR NOT TO PEE

I said nothing. I ran. Yes, I ran. My goal was to get the hell out of there, hope he hadn't seen what I looked like, and hide. Did I mention I was wearing flip-flops? As I was running to the door, I tried to be as quiet as a church mouse. Do you have any idea how hard it is to run quietly in flip-flops and with a large paper shopping bag? It's not impossible! The key is to grip your sandals as hard as you can with your toes so neither a flip nor a flop can be heard. And somehow, the bag cooperated as well and kept its mouth shut. I would pay big money to see that on video.

As I hit the door, I could tell the guy was scrambling to get his pants up, so I knew I didn't have time to make it all the way out of the store; not to mention, it doesn't look good to have a big bag and take off running out the front door of a store. Bit of a red flag. Fortunately, I'm very quick on my feet (pun intended), so I made it to the many racks of men's clothes and quickly pretended to be mesmerized by the shorts hanging on the lowest rack. I was practically kneeling, or more accurately cowering, on the floor "searching for something" as if I had been there all along. That beast came flying around the corner, looking for someone to kill. I'm sure he was embarrassed too, but he looked super-pissed. As his eyes darted around for the culprit, I calmly looked up from my shopping, our eyes met briefly, and I gave the dude a head nod like, "What's up, bro?" Thankfully, he gave the same nod back and kept on searching. Mind you, all this happened in seconds, but it felt like it happened in slow motion. It was nothing short of a miracle that he didn't recognize me, and I'm hoping that he thought it was a little kid who walked in on him, or maybe that he had imagined the whole thing.

When my heart slowed down enough that I couldn't hear it or see it through my shirt, I picked up my bag, walked out to my car and drove home to go to the bathroom. Funny thing about fright; it can either scare the shit out of you, or make you forget you even had to go. Lucky for me, it was the latter.

It goes without saying that family bathrooms have been a fantastic invention. Family bathrooms are the ones where you can go into a single restroom and lock the door. More and more of them are popping up, but not in the numbers most trans people would like. And at times, they are still tough to find, especially in bars and clubs. I guess that makes sense because why would a family with kids be in those places, but when I do find them, it's a relief, literally. As someone who tends to search for and figure out the bathroom situation everywhere I go, I've noticed that more times than not, when I'm waiting for the family bathroom and the door opens up, it's just one person in there, not a family. I imagine that's because it's way more comfortable and private for anyone. If you really think about it, we teach little kids to keep their "privates" private, yet then have males, from little boys up to old guys, whip out their junk in a line in the bathroom. Sure there's a no peeking policy, but it's definitely not a private activity. It's awkward and embarrassing, so family bathrooms have been a nice respite for anyone with any level of restroom anxiety.

I was at a bar in Reno a few years back and had to urinate, so of course, I held it until I couldn't resist it any longer. The bathroom was really small and there wasn't a door on the stall. Are you kidding me? Guys were in and out, using the urinal like a conveyor belt, so apparently, you're just supposed to drop your drawers and go just like that, with everyone watching. Hell, no! I imagine that would be uncomfortable for any guy, trans or not. I didn't know what to do, and I was there with a group of work friends who didn't know my past. What was I supposed to say to them since I just came back from the bathroom? Thankfully, I was a master at making stuff up on the fly, so I told a buddy that I had to run over to the closest casino to use the bathroom because my stomach was jacked up and I didn't want to take a shit in public without a door on the stall. Not entirely a lie, just an embellishment. And as I said before, it's just fine to talk about poop with your buddies, and not many guys would have been comfortable themselves in that situation. So again, my worry and anxiety was for nothing…almost. As I headed out of the bar, my buddy yells, "Hey, wait up; I'll go with you." What? I didn't think guys went to the bathroom together? Turns out he had to take a dump too. Perfect. Here is where my "silent pee" technique really came in handy.

In a perfect world, every public establishment would have a family or unisex bathroom, like the one person restrooms at Starbucks, for example. Times are changing, so that may not be as far-fetched an idea as it seems. I have also heard of gender-neutral restrooms cropping up, though in very limited quantities. These are where both men and women go into the same large restroom or share the sink area. I've personally never seen one, but I have heard that the VIP area of the Body English Nightclub inside the Hard Rock Hotel-Las Vegas has one, and apparently, it was even in a Justin Timberlake/Snoop Dogg music video. Pretty cool. I'm not sure whether or not they are the wave of the future, but my wish is that public restrooms in general could be a much safer place for everyone, regardless of gender.

In the same genre as the bathroom, another place of anxiety for trans people is the locker room. It's like a public restroom on steroids, figuratively, but quite possibly literally. It's bad enough to have to pee in public, but then add to that a larger space where people are also naked. Just when you think things couldn't get any more uncomfortable or awkward. I suspect the majority of guys in a locker room are just as self-conscious or uncomfortable as I am, but the difference is, they can take their clothes off and change without much thought. They may not want to be seen naked either, but they have certain body parts that are expected to be there, so when you are missing a wiener, it's kind of noticeable. Since I've already had top surgery or chest reconstruction, taking my shirt off is easier for me, but many trans guys haven't had that surgery yet or they can't afford to, even though they transitioned many years ago. They still have breasts, so taking their shirts off in a public locker room is not possible. Believe me, I know how blessed I am and I am thankful every day.

For me, taking a shower at the gym is out of the question, even though there are separate shower stalls with curtains. For now, that is too far out of my comfort zone, so I just stink when I leave the gym. That's just another perk of being a guy. If I have to change clothes because I came from work or have some place to be right after, I will plan out my clothes accordingly so I have boxer briefs or workout type underwear on. That way I can change my shorts or pants, but I always have something covering me up. It's a little icky to be wearing sweaty underwear under your clean pants, but that's my best option. I pick a locker that's in a corner, hopefully without close neighbors, and change very quickly. I'm not looking around, so I have no idea whether anyone is watching me, but my guess is no one is. Everyone else is probably too worried that someone is looking at him. Because I'm a worrier and over thinker, I fear someone finding out or that I'll run into someone who knows I'm trans and will tell other people, resulting in my getting kicked out of the locker room. I don't know if that is a legitimate concern or just straight up fear, but I guess I'll deal with that if it ever happens.

Here's something strange I've noticed in the men's locker room, though; there is always some dude who parades around the entire locker room buck-naked. If he happens to have a towel with him, it's over his shoulder and he's just standing around, bending over to pick something up or standing at the sink shaving. Seriously? I guarantee NO ONE wants to see that. And to make matters worse, it's usually the really old or super fat guy or both who doesn't seem to have a care in the world. In a strange way, it's commendable to be that secure with your body, but mostly, it's just gross.

So to sum up, public bathrooms and locker rooms are not a transgender person's best friend, but hopefully, one day they will not be the enemy. I know plenty of trans guys who don't overthink using public restrooms or locker rooms, and frankly, I'm a bit jealous. I have to remember I only began my transition six years ago and I have come a long way. These two places felt overwhelmingly terrifying to go into at first, but now, I head in as if I belong, and the thought of going into the women's room is a foreign concept. I do wonder, though, whether there is a female counterpart in there walking around naked with her towel slung over her shoulder, except now, I imagine she's young and hot. Isn't that what most guys think goes on in the women's locker room?

CHAPTER 9

PAPERWORK AND RED TAPE

*"Go confidently in the direction of your dreams!
Live the life you've imagined."*

— Henry David Thoreau

When non-trans people think of transitioning or someone being transgender, they tend to lump the whole experience into just the physical changes that are visible; they fail to realize all the other changes that are necessary, like the paperwork and documentation. They think "sex change" and that's it. It's easy to forget that with a new name, gender, and identity, the paperwork needs to match, including a driver's license, Social Security card, health documents, etc. The list goes on and on, but eventually, everything needs to change to reflect the new you. It's a daunting task, but somehow, it gets done over time.

In 2008, when I began my transition, I changed my name among my family and friends, but not legally, since I had to be in therapy and have that letter from my therapist stating that I suffered from gender dysphoria. As I've said, the letter wasn't difficult to get, but I wanted to see some actual changes in myself before I tried to change my driver's license. I also wanted to be able to change the gender marker from F to M on my driver's license at the same time, and I wanted to look like a male when I went into the DMV. At this point, I just looked like a very butchy girl. So when I filed the necessary paperwork with the State of Nevada courts to change my name legally, I held onto the completed documents until I was ready.

After about a year into transition, I decided it was time to change my license and make it official. I'm not sure whether I was ready, but I was as ready as I would ever be. I was scared to go to the DMV because I had heard horror stories about other trans people who were humiliated, outed, and denied a new license, but I had the necessary documentation and figured the law was on my side. By now, I was starting to pass as a guy most of the time, so I was more afraid that someone might see my driver's license and wonder why I had some girl's ID. Whenever that did happen, I had to out myself to a complete stranger, which was unpleasant at best.

Even though I was afraid, I forced myself to step up and get the paperwork done. I say "forced" because I had booked a flight a few months in advance and made the reservation under "Jeremy" with the gender marker "male." I had done that on purpose to give myself the nudge to stop procrastinating and get it done. I figured

PAPERWORK AND RED TAPE

I had to get my shit together or I couldn't fly. Since I already had changed my name with the Nevada courts, all I had to do was go to the DMV and Social Security office with my therapist's letter and the letter from my surgeon stating that I had had "any and all necessary gender reconstructive surgeries to complete my transition from female to male."

Clearly, this was not going to be a private matter at the DMV, but I had no choice. Now everyone can agree that the DMV sucks—that's a given—but the thought of sitting there for hours worrying whether I would get someone trans-friendly or not was almost too much to bear. Jayna went with me for support, and we headed out bright and early. First stop DMV. I had triple and quadruple checked that I had the necessary documents that Nevada required so there was no stopping me that day. When we got inside the DMV, no one was in the first line you have to stand in to get a ticket number, but that's not unusual, so I didn't think much of it. We stepped up to the counter and I told the woman enough information for why I was there that she checked my paperwork and handed me a number, just like that. I was so nervous that I honestly don't remember any more.

We headed around the corner to the big waiting room, which literally can hold a few hundred people. I was fully expecting it to be packed to the brim, as it typically was. A trip to the DMV in Las Vegas can easily swallow up four to six hours of your day. As we rounded the corner, the huge waiting area was in full view and only a handful of people were sprinkled around. It was a DMV miracle. I have never had this happen, nor will it probably ever happen again, but my wait time that day was literally thirty seconds. As soon as my butt hit the chair in the waiting room, my number was called. It was like God cleared out the DMV for me, knowing that a lengthy wait was too much for me to handle. It was go time.

We sat down across the counter from the DMV agent who was lucky enough to call my number. To say she was trans-friendly is a bit of a stretch—more like trans-nervous. Of course, this recollection is coming from my perspective, which could be clouded by my fear, worry, panic, and sweat. When I handed over all of my documents, my hand was visibly shaking. I was nervous that I would get turned down because I looked suspicious. I'm not kidding. It felt like she scrutinized my documents for about fifteen minutes, but I'm sure it was more like fifteen seconds. I think I stumped her that day, and she took so long because she didn't know what to do. Next thing I knew, three ladies were now in the mix—all looking at the papers, looking back at the screen, and then looking at me. Like a dork, all I could do each time they glanced at me was flash them a smile. Hell, I must've smiled twenty times, and not because I was happy, nor was it a nice relaxed smile, more like that awful "I'm about to shit myself," forced grin. I began to pray that this experience would end soon and I would leave with a new license.

PAPERWORK AND RED TAPE

Next thing I knew, the first woman, whose desk we were at, began typing, paper-clipped all my documents, put them in her file tray, and asked for the twelve dollars for a new license. I was shocked and relieved. I had brought exactly twelve dollars for this moment, but, of course, I fumbled around for it. With payment in full, she had me look over the document one last time for any errors, and that's when it hit me—I had really done it. Staring back at me on that paper was my new name and my gender marker was an M for male.

I headed over to the photo area, and this time when I grinned, I actually meant it. The photo attendant was the sweetest woman, and, of course, she knew why I was there, because in Nevada, you keep your old driver's license until the new one is mailed out. They put a hole in the old one and you have to carry it, along with a piece of paper that has the new accurate information on it. She looked over the paper I gave her along with my old license, and without skipping a beat, she said, "Okay, Jeremy; let's take your picture." She said that with a smile on her face as well as in her voice. Now the last obstacle was to make sure I didn't use my "I shit my pants" grin. In about seven to ten days, I would find out what kind of smile was captured. We seriously were in and out of that DMV in about thirty-five minutes. And on the way out, I looked up and whispered, "Thank you." God had my back that day for sure.

From there, we headed to the Social Security office, but I wasn't nervous anymore. My driver's license was the most important piece I needed, so that paled in comparison. Oddly enough, when we opened the door to the Social Security Administration, we were the only ones in there too, and I actually thought they were closed, but instead, we were just having a very lucky day. Seriously, within ten minutes, we were back in the car and I had a brand-new Social Security card in hand. FYI, your SS# stays the same, just your name changes.

Jayna and I had cleared our entire day from work to get these two things done, thinking it would take hours at each stop. Instead of going out to celebrate the big day, I went home to take a nap. I had been so nervous and worried that I hadn't slept much the night before. Just curious; has anyone picked up on a theme here? I'm a worrier, and again, true to form, all that worry and loss of sleep was for nothing. I wish I could say I have transitioned out of that character flaw, but unfortunately, I have retained it.

While a driver's license or some form of photo ID is crucial these days, there were a lot of other documents I didn't realize I would want or need to change as well, including my passport, birth certificate, college diploma, and various other cards and accounts. Of all the documents, I have to say changing my passport was the biggest hassle. It's not a secret that postal workers are not the friendliest folks, and yes, I know that's an over-exaggeration, but when I went to my local post office to change my passport, it rang true. Again, I'm not sure whether the guy was confused about what to do, or he didn't agree that I should have the right to change my passport; either way, he was a complete asshole and gave me a lot of negative attitude. But like I said, with the new driver's license in hand, I could handle almost anything. So I didn't budge and my reaction to his attitude made my little bit of nervousness disappear, only to be replaced by anger. I was rude right back and began to tell him my legal rights and what the law said. I have no clue where I found that kind of confidence, but it worked. I over-think things, so of course, I had to replay that day over and over in my mind until I came up with the theory that he had been testing me to see whether I was really man enough, because after all was said and done and I threw the attitude right back at him, he reached out and shook my hand when I left. Odd experience for sure. Or maybe he was just a big douche bag to everyone; one will never know. But if he were just testing me, I passed.

I had read online that changing your birth certificate could be difficult, if not impossible, for a transperson, depending upon your birth state. Michigan at least had information on its state vital statistics website detailing how to get a new birth certificate reflecting a new name and/or gender. So that was a good sign. The directions were a little confusing, but it basically came down to sending in the same information that the DMV required, along with a form my parents could fill out and sign, I guess giving consent. Since I was in my late thirties, I'm not sure that section was necessary, but I wasn't taking a chance, and fortunately, my parents filled it out without hesitation. So off in the mail went my application for an amended birth certificate, my original documents, and of course, the application fee. I sent it via a traceable sender, just to make sure my info made it and wasn't traveling around the world. I tracked it the next few days so I knew when it made it to the State of Michigan Department of Vital Records. I waited and waited a few weeks but heard nothing, so naturally, I worried that my request would be denied. Then about six weeks after sending the documents, I saw my check had been cashed. I took that as a positive sign. Within another couple of weeks, a brand-new birth certificate arrived in the mail. It was awesome. It felt like my true identity was validated and now I had a real document stating what I had always known, that on June 2, 1971, I came into this world as a healthy baby boy named Jeremy.

Other documents and cards may not have been as important as my driver's license and birth certificate, but I wanted everything in my life to reflect the real me. I had had my college diploma on the wall in my office for years, but I took it down when it didn't match me anymore. I was proud of that piece of paper and wanted it back, so I got in touch with the University Colorado registrar, and for a fee, boom, a new diploma to put back on the wall. Over time, I managed to change my name, and if necessary, my gender marker on my gym membership, frequent flyer cards, bills, utilities, and any online profiles. The old me's Facebook account was deleted and Jeremy's emerged. I didn't retain many friends from one account to the other, mostly because I wasn't out to acquaintances from my past and wanted to start fresh. But what's cool is that my friend list began to grow as my family and friends started to find out about me. I even had a few friends from high school who reached out through Facebook. Everyone was awesome, and no one posted anything that would "out" me. It was a great way for my extended family to see my changes from afar, and when we finally got together, it helped ease the anxiety of the "What will he look like?" moment. They could get used to seeing the new me as Jeremy, and finally, see me happy.

It seemed like for a stretch of time, just when I thought I had changed everything, something would come in the mail reminding me that my work wasn't done. I've learned to keep plenty of original documents and letters in my safe. There was a time when I decided I wanted to attend Mortuary School. I applied for financial aid, but I couldn't finish my aid application because, as a male, I had not registered with the selective service. I had never thought about the selective service until that day, and I honestly thought that at my age, it wouldn't matter, but oh, how wrong I was. So I had to register with the selective service and file an exemption before my financial aid could be awarded. I remembered vaguely that young guys eighteen to twenty-five had to register, basically for a database for the government in the event of a military draft, but I never thought it would affect me. For a split second, the thought ran through my head, "Could I be drafted if they started that up again?" Of course not, but I still thought it. I have to give kudos to the selective service agency because on the exemption form, it clearly had transgender as a valid option; I'll be damned. Once that was taken care of and I had my exemption printed out, I could resume my financial aid venture. Even though I didn't stick with that school plan, I can cross off one more rite of passage from my list.

Another area of paperwork and red tape I ran into was with my health insurance. When I first transitioned and changed my name, I had health insurance and the name change wasn't a big deal at all, but changing gender brought on a huge shit storm. My business had an insurance broker, who was very supportive and advised me to leave my gender marker as female for the time being. Having female reproductive parts that require preventative care, coupled with being on testosterone, increased my chances for health problems, so it made more sense to make sure that stuff was covered. That and my insurance carrier could make it very difficult to change my gender marker and deny coverage. So I reluctantly left my gender as female in my medical records.

Boy, did those medical records get awkward the more I passed as a male. My primary doctor knew what was going on, but if I ever had to see someone new, that F in my records always confused the person. For day-to-day stuff like the flu, broken bones, etc., it doesn't really matter what your gender is, but when it comes to gender specific treatments and ailments, that's when it gets complicated and expensive. For example, if I had changed my gender marker to male, and God forbid, anything had gone wrong with my female parts, I would have had to pay out-of-pocket because a guy wouldn't have those organs or have those things happen, according to my insurance company. On the same note, my testosterone prescription wasn't covered because a female wouldn't be taking that drug. It is definitely a catch-22 scenario that many transgender people have to deal with.

This insurance situation made me keep thinking of the 2001 documentary *Southern Comfort* that follows the last year of Robert Eads' life. He was a trans man who was diagnosed with ovarian cancer, but he was turned down for treatment by many doctors; because of a lack of health care, he succumbed to cancer. This is a reality for transgender men and women who die from preventable and treatable diseases. It's a horrific tragedy. I didn't want to be a statistic like that, so leaving my health insurance as female seemed worth it. And that was well and good when I had insurance, but after my family sold our company, my health insurance went away. My insurance broker tried to help me apply for individual plans, but as he warned me could happen, I was denied coverage because of my transgender status, which was considered a pre-existing condition. Well, duh! Not having health insurance is really frightening, but that too is just a harsh reality in the transgender community.

Fortunately, times are changing, though slowly. Because of the Affordable Care Act or Obamacare, I can't be turned down for coverage due to any pre-existing condition, even being transgender. But they sure can jack up the premium costs and make sure that trans-related care is exempt. That too is starting to change, and a few states like California are making great strides in covering transgender folks. But naturally, I don't live in those states, and while I may be able to get insurance, like most Americans trans or not, I can't afford the monthly cost. So back to square one.

The one saving grace was when I moved back to Colorado for a couple of years; I found an amazing doctor and medical practice, North Vista Medical. I stumbled upon Dr. David Tusek and his practice by doing a Google search for any doctors in the Boulder/Denver area who accepted patients without insurance. I clicked on North Vista Medical's website because it had a few locations in the area, and one of them was only ten minutes from my house. It offered a low-cost alternative to health insurance called Nextera Healthcare, which is basically a health membership. According to the website, Nextera "offers primary care programs for individuals, couples, families and businesses, and is an effective option for those looking for a complete primary care program…." It's an all-inclusive practice and provides exceptional preventative care that cuts down on the likelihood of needing ER visits.

I wasn't too worried about something big happening like getting hit by a bus because hospitals have to treat people who come in with trauma, but I was concerned that without health insurance, I wouldn't be able to afford any preventative care or doctor visits for the little stuff, so this was the perfect answer for me. For a very low monthly fee, I had unlimited office visits, direct access to my doctor, and finally, I felt like I was in good hands. With Nextera, all labs, x-rays, etc., are at a much lower negotiated cost, so whatever I would need to stay healthy wouldn't bankrupt me. Nextera and North Vista Medical's websites and contact information are located in the Resources section at the end of this book, and I strongly urge everyone to check them out.

I was a patient at North Vista Medical for quite a while without disclosing I was transgender, partly because it didn't matter at the time, but mostly because I was fearful of the staff's reaction. However, my testosterone prescription from my old doctor in Las Vegas was about to run out and I didn't have any refills, so I didn't have much of a choice but to disclose my status or go back to Vegas for a visit. I decided to make an appointment to see Dr. Tusek and thought to myself, "If he has a problem with it, we had a good run." When he came in the room, we briefly chatted about how life and work were going, and then I told him, "The only reason I came in today is to share a little more about my medical history; I am transgender." His reaction was priceless. He sat back in his chair, settled in, and said, "That's fantastic; thank you for sharing that with me." Boom, done!

Unknown to me, Dr. Tusek and his entire practice had a lot of experience and expertise in hormone therapy. Not for transgender patients specifically, but as he said, that didn't matter. Patients were patients, and his practice was there to help and treat everyone. Holy shit, where had this doctor been my whole life? For the first time in my transition, I finally felt like I had a doctor who really understood me, and I knew I was in the best hands possible. We hit the ground running to make sure I was the healthiest I could be and that my hormone levels, not just testosterone, were in order. Again, my relief was palpable. Dr. Tusek was the one who suggested I try out the testosterone implant instead of self-injections, and I was definitely on board with that. Even though I have moved back to Las Vegas, I have kept my Nextera membership because I'm not losing that level of care. The cool thing is that Dr. Tusek is still accessible via phone, text, or Skype, and yes, it is expensive to travel back to Colorado a couple of times a year to have my implant replaced, but that cost doesn't even compare to the insurance premiums I would pay for crappy health coverage, not to mention, the comfort of knowing I can be open about myself and that my doctor and his entire staff really care about my wellbeing; that's worth every penny. It's not uncommon to get a text from my doctor, just checking to see how I'm doing, and I know for sure I never had that level of healthcare before.

CHAPTER 10

FEARING FEAR

*"People will hate you, rate you, shake you, and break you.
But how strong you stand, is what makes you."*

— Author Unknown

I've had people say to me things like, "You're so brave," "Look what you've overcome," and "How could you be afraid of anything anymore?" And in theory, they have a point. I hated my life as it was, so I decided to make a big change, whether anyone liked it or not. I didn't talk a big game; I just transformed in front of everyone and chose life. Is that courageous? I don't know; it was just survival. Change was my only option if I wanted to live and finally be happy. And even though I knew I had the strength, deep down, fear is still ever present.

Most of my fears are not based on past negative experiences, but more about future worries—the "what ifs." If I look back over my life, I can't find one instance where the what-if scenario either came true or was as bad as I had built it up to be. Yet, somehow, I still struggle with worry and fear, whether it's unfounded or not.

The fear started out as, "What if I can't pull this off and I'm stuck in some kind of gender limbo for the rest of my life?" Then the worry was, "When will I start to pass as a guy full-time and stop worrying?" But the worry didn't go away; it just morphed into, "What if someone finds out?" All of those what-ifs were completely beyond my control, and would it matter if any or all of them came true? But for someone who is a natural born worrier, this line of questioning was ever present in my mind.

Early in transition, as I've said before, I wanted instant gratification and wanted to wake up one morning looking, walking, and talking like a man, kind of like Tom Hanks in the movie *Big* when he wishes on a carnival game that he was big, and the next morning, he wakes up a full-grown adult male. While that made for a great movie, in hindsight I'm glad real-life transition doesn't work that way. It would be pretty strange to go to bed one night as a girl and wake up the next as a man, and I'm pretty sure everyone would notice and freak out, including myself. It's called transition for a reason!

Over time, as I have settled into transitioning and gained more self-confidence, the worry and fear has begun to simmer down, and fortunately, I have great family members and friends who help keep me in check. They all know how to remind me that everything is okay and it's just my anxiety acting up.

As I mentioned in the last chapter, I had put a deadline on myself to change my legal name and gender marker because of my travel plans. But when that vacation finally came, I was scared to death to fly. The, "Will I pull this off and genuinely pass as a guy?" question was put to the test when that travel day arrived. With my boarding pass and new driver's license in hand, I waited in the endless security line at the airport, and of course, I was sweating. This was the first time that new license was going to be scrutinized, not because I was transgender, but because that's what TSA agents do; regardless, I naturally took it personally. When it was finally my turn to hand over my ID and boarding pass to the TSA guy, my guess is that I looked suspiciously nervous. Being sweaty, shaky, and with eyes darting around to see whether anyone was on to me, all while trying to get through airport security, is not recommended. The agent looked at my ID over and over, looked at me a couple of times, and then—I read it as "reluctantly"—stamped the boarding pass and handed my stuff back to me. I had made it through…almost.

I made it about three steps when he called me back. This was it! My mind went from zero to panic, and it felt like all the what-ifs were about to come true. I'm not sure where my reaction came from, but without even thinking, I turned around quickly and glared at the guy as if to say, "What the hell do you want?" Of course, I didn't actually say anything. He asked for my license and boarding pass again so I shoved it back at him and muttered, "What's the problem?" in a low pissed off tone. Probably not super smart, but that's just how it came out. I thought, "If I'm going down, I'm going down with a fight." As he looked over the documents again, I just focused on him, like I was about to pounce. Maybe he took it as I was just annoyed to be delayed or maybe he thought I was just another one of the assholes who came through his line daily, but for some reason, my reaction seemed to throw him off a bit (me too); he handed me back my license and boarding pass and said, "Have a good flight."

Was this interaction about me being transgender? Who knows, but of course, I thought so. Only years later did I even entertain the thought that it could be something else. The fact that I was nervous, sweating, and kept looking around definitely could've been the problem, or maybe my boarding pass was randomly selected for additional screening. I'll never know, but I will never forget how terrified I was. In that moment, my mind went on a complete irrational tangent; I was going to be pulled aside, questioned, outed, strip-searched, and arrested. Yeah, right! I've got to stop watching *Locked Up Abroad* on the National Geographic Channel. The fear of being publicly outed and humiliated isn't far-fetched because that does happen to trans people, but I need to stop being so defensive and fearful that it's always going to happen to me, and just relax. In fact, I have never even come close to being outed and shamed, so again, I have no basis for my worry. Unfortunately, I create my fears and anxieties to the point where I can convince myself they are real. I waste a lot of time and energy worrying, but it never comes to fruition how I had imagined.

I have been fearful, and at times still am, of losing friends and extended family once they find out about my transition. This fear kind of baffles me because when I decided to take the leap of faith and become the man I knew I was, in that moment, I didn't care who I lost or how anyone felt; I only cared about being true to myself for once. Once I made those changes, that strong conviction and confidence waned and I worried what other people thought about me and whether or not they would leave me. Again, that was not based on any past experiences of rejection, and in fact, I haven't lost anyone solely because I am transgender.

Only two people are no longer in my life after transitioning, but that was my choice. My transition was difficult on these "friends," and time after time, they would "slip" in crowds of people and call me by the wrong name, always referring to me as "she" or "her" and then laugh it off, as if it were no big deal. It was clear they were very uncomfortable around me, and even when I explained that all of those slips hurt me and could actually put me in danger, their behavior never changed. They treated my transitioning as a joke, so I cut them out of my life. They were no longer healthy for me, and frankly, I didn't have to take that crap anymore. Of course, it was a difficult and sad decision to separate myself, but now I see it as empowering. I definitely found out who my true friends were and no one should ever have to put up with being called a freak, even if it's disguised as a simple joke. Those who really cared about me did an amazing job of using my new name and gender, and slips are natural and to be expected, especially in the early stages, but there's a difference between a slip and flat out refusing to change your thinking. I didn't have room in my new, happy life for anyone who wasn't supportive and who genuinely wouldn't try to transition with me.

Through my transition, I have gained much better friends, and by opening up and being authentic, my friendships have grown deeper. Even though, rationally, I understand that it doesn't matter what anyone else thinks of me, the fear of rejection and judgment does still enter my mind. As long as I stay focused on the wonderful people who are by my side, no matter what, I can work through my fears and get back to my original mentality that I transitioned for me and me alone. Of course, by writing this book, I will "out" myself, but for once, I feel completely different because I'm choosing full disclosure, have control of my information, and have talked this through at length with my core support system. Not to mention, I am finally ready.

Being outed by someone is a constant fear, especially if it's done unexpectedly and I'm not prepared. And sometimes, I wonder whether I am obligated to tell someone. This is something I wrestle with, and if I am obligated, then who needs to know, and when do I disclose? Once I passed as male 100 percent of the time, I chose to live by stealth, which meant I didn't tell anyone about my past and blended into society as just another dude. No one would have guessed that I was born as a female; that's what I thought I wanted, and honestly, to a degree, I still do. I wish gender didn't matter at all, but that's not the world we live in. Everyone has a natural curiosity and wants to know what category someone fits in—boy or girl. That's usually the first question someone asks when a baby is born, "What did you have?" So once I started my journey, all I wanted was just to be a guy and fit in.

I have enjoyed disappearing into a male life and building new friendships and work relationships as Jeremy without disclosing anything else. I want people to get to know me, the guy. Blending in as just another average Joe has been amazing, and my confidence and self-esteem is much better, but going stealth has also been lonely and isolating. I guess, "Be careful what you wish for" applies here. As I grow and mature into manhood, I've realized that there is much more to me than meets the eye, and I'm finally at a place in my life where I'm not ashamed of my past. How I became a man may differ from most, but I am a better man for it.

So the question again, "Do I have to tell people about my trans status?" The answer I've come to terms with is a simple, "NO." I'm not obligated or required to disclose my past or my medical history to anyone, with a couple of exceptions, like the IRS, Social Security, DMV, etc. Basically, when anyone needs to pull up my Social Security number, my old name will show up and then I will have to clear up that mess, or if I go to a doctor and feel it necessary information for proper treatment, I will disclose. I don't necessarily have to disclose anything on a job application; however, if the employer ran a background check, my old name would pop up, but it's pretty easy to laugh that off as a mistake.

In most of those instances, it was never a big deal, just uncomfortable. But digging a bit deeper, as I built new relationships with people, and as they shared their life experiences with me, I would feel guilty for holding back. I've never been good at forming deep, healthy friendships because I'm so used to keeping people at arm's length, but I have really wanted to change that, which ties into my dilemma. My experience has been that when I do disclose my past, relationships get better and stronger, and people feel like they can trust me more because I trusted them with my secret; however, I still hesitate and stew about whom I tell and when.

But the initial friendship-building period where I try to share parts of myself, except that I used to be a girl, is exhausting. I can't share just any story from childhood; for instance, if the group were talking about having to wear dresses as a little girl, and I chimed in, without thinking, that I hated them too, it would get a little awkward. Until this book, I never shared old photos with anyone or had any around the house because why would a little boy be photographed in a figure skating dress? I was constantly changing my stories or omitting details that would out me. And sometimes, I would make up stories just to fit in. Buffering or censoring what

I shared was difficult to keep track of, and I'm tired of doing it. It's such a relief when I'm talking or hanging out with people who know my whole story so I can just relax and be myself. I can say anything, share anything, and honestly, sometimes tossing in a story or comment about my old self is funny and tends to put people at ease.

So I've established that I'm not obligated to tell anyone, but as I said before, living a stealth lifestyle and constantly censoring myself has been lonely. I've come to realize that I have my entire family and a large group of friends who are a true support system, so if I tell someone who doesn't like it, I didn't need that person anyway. All of the worry and fear I have put into this is wasted and is basically giving my power and control away to others who don't matter. Most people want to be liked, and I'm definitely no exception. I like everyone around me to get along, and I avoid conflict like it's the plague. It truly comes down to the fear of someone not liking me anymore and rejecting me.

Sometimes, to achieve homeostasis, I put the needs and wants of others ahead of my own when those people usually don't deserve it or probably never asked me to, and what I'm slowly starting to figure out is that very few people reciprocate. As they say on airplanes, "Put your own oxygen mask on first before helping anyone else." That logic definitely applies to life. I need to learn to take care of myself first, do what makes me happy and allows me to live an honest and authentic life, and forget the haters. Easier said than done, especially for a gifted and practicing worrier, but since years of practice helped me to perfect my anxiety, my guess is that many more years of practicing to let things go and stop creating the negative what-ifs will pay off. I have wasted enough valuable time on that kind of nonsense.

Before I started writing this book, I bought a book by Patrick Snow, titled, *Creating Your Own Destiny*. I had the book for nearly two years and would skim through it now and then when I was trying to figure out what I wanted to do for my next career. Throughout his book, Patrick said to do what you are passionate about. And he said he was a publishing and book marketing coach, so if you would just reach out to him, he was ready to help anyone make his or her dream of writing a book and having a speaking career a reality. Basically, he was coaching people on how to create your own career and fulfill your true destiny.

I had always entertained the thought of writing a book about my transition, and I even had friends try to coax me into doing so, usually after I had shared a funny story like peeing my pants, but I never thought I could or would be ready to share my story with strangers. But one day I figured, "Why not?" Patrick's contact information was in the book, so I emailed him and asked for his guidance. I honestly never thought I would hear back, or at best, I thought I would get some sort of form email thanking me for buying his book, but within a day or two, he called me. I was so shocked; I couldn't believe this International Best-Selling author and speaker called me! I have to say it felt pretty cool, and as we chatted, I started to believe that I could actually write a book.

Patrick asked me a little bit about myself, what I did for a living, you know, the typical "Who are you?" questions. And I had a ton of questions for him like, "Do you have to be a great writer? How do you even start the process?" and on and on. And it came down to a simple answer, "Anyone is capable of writing a book," and he was willing to share his expertise and guidance to help me get it done. The biggest question he had for me was, "Do you have the discipline and determination to do it?" and "Are you passionate about the book subject?" If so, he said he would take me on as his client and help me every step of the way. I'm sure there were other things that he looked for in a client, but that was what stuck with me. This wasn't one of those too good to be true moments because he was offering his coaching and mentoring services, but I actually had do the writing. I had a big task ahead, and I was the only one who could commit to doing the work.

I was excited and wanted to go after making my own career and future, but fear reared its ugly head once again, so I didn't tell Patrick my idea of writing about my journey and myself. Instead, we talked about the business that I used to own and all of my experience with franchising and sales. The next thing I knew, Patrick and

I were brainstorming about topics related to my past career, which by the way, I was not passionate about.

I didn't share my truth with Patrick, and there was no way he would have ever known, so I kept quiet and went with the flow. My rationale was, "Well, if I'm not ready to tell a stranger on the phone who I really am and what I want to write about, I must not be ready to publish that book for the world to see." There's truth in that line of thinking, but it felt more like a cop-out to me. But I was still excited, and after our twenty-minute chat, I signed up. Patrick Snow was now my writing, publishing, and speaking coach, and I began the process of writing a franchising book. We dove right in within a matter of weeks, and before I knew it, I had five chapters under my belt and had resigned myself to the fact that I would finish this book, give speaking to businesses and franchise groups my best shot, and one day learn to be passionate about it. Not exactly creating the destiny I wanted, but a destiny I was lukewarm about. How crazy is that? That is not logic; that's fear, plain and simple.

For the next six months or so, I worked on my business book here and there, never giving it my full attention, and I found jobs to keep me busy, hoping they would take the place of having to finish that book altogether. All the while, I was wanting to write about something I was clearly passionate about, which was me. The lonelier I felt, the more I wanted to write this book because I knew it was important to tell my story in a candid and funny way that would hopefully resonate with someone going through the same thing; maybe I could prevent someone else from feeling as lonely and isolated as I was. And I also wanted to let people know that it was okay to laugh at some of the things that occur during the transformative process.

So in January, 2014, I put my business book aside and applied the writing formula I had learned from Patrick to a new book, which is the one you are reading now. I found the time to write, mostly on my days off or in the evenings, and I began to make significant progress. I was getting excited and picked up momentum, so I finally told a few friends what I was writing about. It wasn't until I had about eight chapters completed that I knew I needed to tell Patrick I'd changed books on him. I needed his help, and that's what I had signed up for—that and it wasn't fair to either of us to put this off any longer.

Fearing what his response might be, I called Patrick and said, "Hey, I've decided to write a different book, something that's near and dear to my heart, and on a topic I want to build my speaking career around. I don't want to write a business book anymore, and for the last six or seven months, I've actually been writing about my life as a transgender man." Then I waited for his response, which was quick. "That's great! You have to write about your passion." That was it, no judgment, no rejection, no, "I don't want to work with you anymore"; instead, "Let's dig in and get this done."

He was surprised that I was afraid to tell him; in fact, that's the reaction most people have. Not having to or thinking that I have to create my destiny by myself has lightened the load and removed my self-created burden.

After that day, my writing took off and my excitement for my future grew exponentially. Speaking my truth and asking for help has paid off in so many ways, and I am eternally grateful. Now that the "Me" book was in full motion, I started thinking about the future and wondering whether, if this book were a success, was there anyone in my life whom I would want to hear that I'm transgender directly from my mouth versus finding out from someone else. For once, a what-if wasn't a negative. And there were a few people. It didn't feel like obligation anymore; I truly cared about these friends and the relationships we had cultivated so much that it would break my heart if they heard the news secondhand. I didn't want them ever to think that I didn't trust them enough to share my true self with them. So I set out on a mission to share my truth with the last few who didn't know—those friends who allowed me into their lives completely, so I wanted to return the favor. As nerve-wracking as it was, the truth set me free.

Whether it's telling my truth or just living it, when it's out there, I feel better. My fears are so rooted in hiding and keeping things from others that I've had to break those terrible habits. Worries stay hidden inside and start to fester and grow into wild assumptions. Next thing I know, I've got myself so worked up and actually believing the assumptions I've made about what others think of me that I almost become paralyzed with fear. And so far, my assumptions are always wrong. Because I've heard stories of bad things happening to other trans people, I've taken that fear on and have almost sat back and waited for those things to happen to me. That's not living; it's waiting. Instead of having the mindset that I'm going to be okay, I've almost missed the fact that I already am okay, and I have a network of people who have my back no matter what. To quote Dr. Seuss, "Be who you are and say what you feel because those who mind don't matter and those who matter don't mind." I can't think of better advice than that.

CHAPTER 11

PUTTING THE PIECES TOGETHER

*"Today you are you, that is truer than true.
There is no one alive who is youer than you."*

— Dr. Seuss

I've mentioned throughout this book the different places I've lived, but I have not always elaborated on why or how I moved around so much, most of which was going back and forth between Las Vegas and Boulder. Not that my geographical whereabouts matter, but all that moving and each location has played a key role in my transition, allowing me to let go of the past and embrace the future.

In an earlier chapter, I explained that I went to college in Boulder, at the University of Colorado. It wasn't the most profound college experience, but I have nothing to compare it to, so I guess it was just right. I stayed in Boulder for a number of years after graduation, went to massage school, and most importantly, met three of the most significant people in my life: Gerald, Jennifer, and Belinda. These three friendships were crucial to me because they helped me grow into a better person, to become self-sufficient, and to learn to live on my own, which up until then, I didn't know how to do. Leaving Boulder in 1998 was difficult, but honestly, I could no longer afford to stay and was offered an opportunity to start a business with my family in Las Vegas. Painting houses, working at a hardware store, and dabbling with a massage career just wasn't cutting it anymore, and it was time for me to grow up even more.

So for the next fourteen years, I lived in fabulous Las Vegas, Nevada. During that time, my family and I owned a successful haircare franchising business. That career afforded me opportunities I never would have had otherwise, and through it, I built many amazing friendships that I still have today. Unfortunately, I spent so much time living in the past, wishing and incessantly talking about going back to Colorado, that I'm sure my friends in Las Vegas were sick of hearing about Boulder. I had such fond memories of my time there, and I always thought that the grass was greener on the other side of the fence. I can honestly say that when I lived in Boulder, right after college, I was genuinely as happy as I could be. Not that I liked myself during that time, but I was so busy with my friends that I was distracted from my self-loathing. It was also the first time I had cultivated true and meaningful friendships.

Once I transitioned and my family sold its business, nothing was really holding me back from trying out Boulder from a new, male perspective. I was finally in a financially sound position to make the move, and I thought going back would tie up loose ends and bring me happiness again. I figured, "Why not go back to a place I loved, as the person I love?" So I decided to make that dream a reality. I reached out to my friends Gerald and Belinda, who were still living in the area with their families, and I told them I was coming back. Unfortunately for me, Jennifer had moved to the Boston area some years back, but we continue to do our best to keep in touch long distance; thankfully, there's Facebook.

I got connected with a realtor in the Boulder area, and we started the house hunt over the phone and Internet. I quickly realized that not much had changed over the last fourteen years; I still couldn't afford to live in Boulder, so I would have to settle for the suburbs. Fortunately, I loved the whole area, so it wasn't much of a sacrifice. The home buying process was exciting, but it was pretty stressful to try to find the right home when I didn't even live in the state yet. I couldn't afford to make numerous trips back and forth just to look at houses, so I only flew in once for a period of three days, met my realtor Chris for the first time, and looked at close to thirty houses. We definitely saw some stinkers, and at the end of those three days, I went back to Nevada empty-handed.

We kept up the search online, and I knew I would eventually find the right house, but I was also running into a problem finding a mortgage lender that was willing to fund that dream. Not so easy. For a while, it seemed like my dream would be squished because lender after lender all said no. Even though I had money in the bank, I didn't have a job, so taking me on was too much of a risk. Rationally, that made sense, but I was so frustrated. I guess lenders can't take your word for it that you won't spend all your savings and default on your loan. I wasn't about to pay for the house outright because then I would be flat broke and couldn't eat.

But by the grace of God, Chris mentioned that he had just met a mortgage loan officer named Karen who had come in to speak to his real estate firm a week earlier. Even though he had not worked directly with her yet, he passed along her information to me and felt confident that she would be able to help me out. And so I made the call. Right from the very first phone conversation I had with her, I knew one thing for sure; Karen would exhaust all possibilities and leave no stone unturned to help me. And lucky for me, she was a miracle worker and I was pre-approved for a home loan.

When I started the loan process with her over the phone, I didn't disclose that I was transgender, nor did I tell my realtor. I stalled until I actually found the house I wanted and had to do the full loan application. I figured, "Why out myself prematurely, right? If I don't find a house or am not approved, why should I tell her?" I had a little window of time before we got deep into the loan process and I would have to give her my Social Security number. I had to find a home first. Then two days before Thanksgiving, I saw the perfect listing online and quickly called Chris. He ran out and previewed the house for me that same day, and I told him as long as it was structurally fine and didn't stink, I'd take it. That was really my criteria. We had gone into a similar home with the same floor plan when I visited, so that was good enough for me. Apparently, most people don't buy homes sight unseen, but I just had a gut feeling that this was my house. I reassured Chris that I was really okay not previewing the home myself and we put in an offer.

Of course, now I would have to give Karen more information about myself because I knew once she pulled my Social Security number, my old name would come up on my credit report. It was only a matter of time before she would ask who Jennifer was because everyone always did. So once the sellers accepted the purchase offer, it was time to start the lengthy loan process. So, as I was driving one day, Karen called to finish up with some of the application paperwork, so I figured, "Today's the day." Just to be clear, I had Bluetooth in my car so the call came through the radio. Just wanted to mention that so when my mom reads this, she won't think I was texting and driving. We exchanged the typical pleasantries, but I knew what was coming next, and I was already uncomfortable. Fear is so irrational and stupid. My mind raced to, "What if I get turned down for a loan because I'm transgender? What if she freaks out and doesn't want to help me? What if, what if?" My mind went right to the "what if" scenarios, as is customary for me, and I didn't even consider staying calm and having the attitude of, "Hey, I'm a kickass guy who happens to be trans; deal with it." Nope, I went straight for my bread-and-butter move—worry!

Somehow, the conversation took a really weird turn, thanks to me. Karen was reading the loan application verbatim, just so we wouldn't miss anything, and she asked me my name, date of birth, sex…and that's when I freaked out. Why would she ask me what my sex was? Was there a question about my gender; could she tell from the phone conversations? Was I regressing and no longer passed as a guy? Believe it or not, all of these questions ran through my mind in the same amount of time it took me to say, "What?" She repeated, "Sex?" And by now, my fear turned to panic. I could hear my heart beating loudly. Why this threw me off, I don't know, because I was already going to tell her, but I imagined it going much smoother than that.

Now I had taken too much time to answer and couldn't ask "What?" again because that would be stupid. But what came out of my mouth next was even dumber and made me laugh. I responded by saying, "Fax? I don't have a fax machine." Really? What the hell was I talking about? Clearly, Karen had no idea either. Now it was her turn to ask, "What? No, I said, 'Sex,' as in male or female." I laughed and told her that I thought she had asked me for my fax and we shared a nice giggle. Well, with a segue like that, it was go time. So I said, "Hey, now that we're talking about it, there is something I need to tell you before you run my Social. Another name is going to come up and it belongs to me. I used to be a girl."

Now, I was expecting silence or a stutter at this point, but not with Karen. Without skipping a beat, the first thing she said was, "You know that has nothing to do with a home loan, don't you?" Is that not the best response ever? To be honest, I didn't know that. That's what I had hoped, but I had made being transgender such a big deal in my head that I assumed it was a big deal in everything. We finished the questions for the loan and I thanked her for being so cool with me. She told me she was raised in Boulder, which is a very open and inclusive town, and it just wasn't a big deal. This conversation reaffirmed my longing to move back. Without Karen's help, I wouldn't have been able to pull it off. I knew that renting in the Boulder area wasn't something I could afford for very long, and at the time, interest rates were super low, which meant a mortgage was my only affordable option. With the teamwork of Chris and Karen, they made another dream come true for me.

All the chatter about Colorado was over; I was moving back. It was wonderful to be back among my old friends, and we got to know each other better, as adults. For the next fifteen months, I learned so much about myself, and I realized that the grass is never greener on the other side, nor can you go back and re-create past experiences. Nothing is ever the same. I surely wasn't the same person going back to Boulder, and my friends had different lives as well, all of which was positive, but difficult for me to adjust to. I had visions of picking up where we had left off, but fourteen years is a long time. I enjoyed fixing up my house, but I always felt like it should have a family in it, not a lonely bachelor. I made myself a man cave, decked out with all of my sports memorabilia, an air hockey table, and just manly crap. It was awesome, but empty. I even broke out my old hockey trophies to display proudly. I quickly realized that they all had my old name on them, so instead of putting them back in the box, I decided to have all the nameplates redone with "Jeremy" on them. It felt great to have a part of my past on display without bringing attention to the old me.

It was all coming together, almost. I still kept everyone at a distance, and I found it difficult to meet new friends. I had trouble letting my guard down, and I was torn between hiding my past or sharing it, so I kept to myself. I had this great house with a great man cave, and I was turning into a hermit again. I made a few new friends and was trying to start a new life, but I chose not to tell these friends about myself. It was like I wanted to relive my past experiences of living in Colorado, but I didn't want anyone to find out who I used to be when I lived there. That became a very difficult task because I was back to censoring myself. I would meet other people who went to college there, and without thinking, I would get excited and talk about playing hockey for CU, but then realize I would have to lie and tell them I played on the men's team. On the surface, that might not seem like a big deal, except it's a small community so someone would end up asking me whether I had played with so-and-so whom they knew had played on the team around the same time I would have. So much for starting over; I was back to lying and hiding. I really thought I wanted a true stealth lifestyle and to forget who I used to be, but that was easier said than done. And it turns out, not realistic for me. If I wanted to start fresh, I should have chosen a place where I didn't have any past attachments—live and learn.

I decided that reconnecting with a bit of my past might help, so I looked up my old friend, Sandi Daileda, from massage school. We had lost contact once I moved to Las Vegas the first time, but I had always thought of her. We hadn't been close friends in massage school, but I always felt a real connection with her, and knowing she was still in Boulder, I knew I needed to reach out. When I had left, she had been a cranial sacral therapist, and I remembered how grounded and relaxed I felt each time she worked on me, so I thought I could use a bit of that now. Thanks to Facebook, I found Sandi and reached out to her the safe way—by email. I sent a message to her, explaining who I used to be, to jog her memory, and who I was now and that I hoped we could reconnect.

Within a few days, Sandi responded and we made plans to get together. I was nervous to see her again because so much time had passed and I was so different, but once we got together, it was like we picked up right where we had left off. Because of Sandi's gentle and nurturing soul, I knew she would be more than fine with my transition, and as luck would have it, she was still in the bodywork industry, but on an even bigger scale. Sandi now had her own Super Healing Arts Center in Boulder and specialized in not only massage and cranio-sacral therapy, but she also encompassed her gifts of being clairvoyant—a multi-sensory intuitive and psychic medium—into her practice. Combining all of these skills and many more, Sandi performs healing treatments, as well as guides others to heal themselves. Her healing sessions release data and past experiences or memories that we hang onto; whether it's traumatic or just out-dated thinking, this information just isn't necessary to keep in our bodies anymore. When that "junk" is released, it frees up the data memory in the body and allows a person finally to see the gifts and potential that have been buried. No longer is it necessary to trip over past experiences and hang onto old, destructive ways of thinking. I was very interested in having a healing session with Sandi, not only because I missed being around bodywork, but I also intuitively knew that I needed it. I could use a bit of spiritual spring cleaning and grounding for sure.

As we chatted and caught up, Sandi and I both felt like we were meant to reconnect. Being around Sandi, whether for tea as friends or receiving actual healing sessions, I could start to feel myself change for the better, meaning I was allowing myself to be more present in the moment, more grounded. Somehow, all of my sessions with Sandi always came back to the topic of me being transgender, not in a narcissistic way, but in the sense that I needed to embrace it as my journey, my true story, and my identity. She picked up immediately on my internal struggle between the two lives and my apprehension of acknowledging my past and redefining my future. She was the one who told me it was necessary and healthy to embrace both and to be gentle with myself. Each time we met, we would work on my releasing my female energy and embracing or welcoming the male.

Sandi would always mention during these sessions that she saw me doing something that encompassed my transition; in terms of a career, my job would be about me in some way. I brushed that off time and again, mostly because it brought up fear and anxiety, and it went against my desire to hide. She never said what that career would be or would look like specifically, but it had to do with being open and comfortable with myself, and that I would give something back to the transgender community. I really didn't want to hear that at the time, and I wasn't ready or sure I ever would be. So instead, we would concentrate on healing the disconnect between my male and female energy, helping the old me to let go and the new me to stand tall. I attribute so much of my growth as a person to Sandi. Not to mention she was able to get my restless leg syndrome under control for the first time in twenty-five years; sleeping well is priceless. I came out of each of our sessions feeling rejuvenated, calm, and grounded, and I could feel my confidence as a man strengthen. Having such an amazing, beautiful friend to help fine-tune this journey has been a pure blessing.

No matter where I was or what job I was doing, I couldn't stop thinking about what Sandi had said—that my future career may have something to do with my story. Whether she meant directly or indirectly, I didn't know, but maybe it was more about not hiding as much and letting more people know me completely. Even though I took to heart what she said, I continued to play it safe and go stealth. But the struggle of keeping my past hidden was finally taking a toll and I was exhausted. I was starting to crave a more authentic and honest life—whatever that meant, I knew it wasn't what I was currently living. I missed being around people like me, those who really knew the struggles and triumphs of transition, so I decided to step outside of my comfort zone and go to a trans guy support group in Denver. I was really apprehensive at first, thinking, "Will I fit in? Will I be trans enough?" And other weird thoughts. You may be wondering how a transgender man like myself could even question whether I was trans enough for a support group; well, logically, of course, I'm enough, but illogically, it's something many trans people think about. That feeling of, "What if everyone in the group transitioned decades ago or looks way more manly, whatever that looks like, and I don't fit in?" Never have I been to a support group where I wasn't accepted, no matter what stage of transition I was in, but the what-if chatter in my head was back with a vengeance. And this group was no different than any other group I had been to, meaning I fit in just fine.

Each time I went to the group, my nerves calmed down and I enjoyed being surrounded by my community. To hear similar stories to mine and different takes on transition made me feel more relaxed and better about myself. I felt at home being in a group of trans guys who encompassed the whole spectrum, from those who may have just muttered the words, "I'm transgender" out loud for the first time, to the veterans who had been walking this journey for many years. Every single person had so much to offer this group. The old timers could share their experiences and wisdom, while the youngsters (early in transition) could ask questions and remind all of us what early transition was like—the good, the bad, and the ugly. I know I was in a rush to get through that early stage, so I missed focusing on the details; listening to others helped to bring some of that back.

From this group experience, I decided to take another step and sign up for the group facilitator training that The Center offered. I'm not sure where this newfound confidence came from, and frankly, I was shocked I signed up. The class was awesome and gave me a brand new appreciation and respect for support group facilitators; that job is a lot tougher than it looks. Leading a group and making sure everyone who wants to be heard is heard and respected, all while providing a safe space, isn't easy. Hats off to those who make it look effortless. I co-facilitated one meeting and was looking forward to helping out when necessary, but while all this was happening, I was becoming more and more restless and was entertaining the notion of moving, once again.

I was enjoying being around the transgender community again, but I didn't tell my friends that I was going to the Friday night groups, and I made sure my stealth persona and my out life never crossed paths. I was back to living a double life. It was becoming clear that I missed being in an environment where everyone knew my past and present. I missed my community of friends in Las Vegas, the place where I had transitioned and where I had a large number of people who were there for the entire journey.

Over time, I'm sure I could have "come out" to everyone around me in Boulder and created that community of support, but I wanted to go back to the community I had already built. Fourteen years had been a long time to cultivate incredible friendships, and it took leaving Las Vegas to realize how much I needed and appreciated those friends. Las Vegas was the place where I had experienced my toughest times and survived. It was there that I let Jenny go and that Jeremy had begun. It had more meaning to me than I realized—it was my home. The old saying, "Home is where the heart is," is really true. So, over the river and through the woods, back to Las Vegas I would go.

For the third time, my stuff would make a road trip between Colorado and Nevada. Too bad moving companies don't have a frequent user program. I had fixed up my house a bit and unintentionally flipped it enough that it added quite a bit of value in fifteen months. Chris was able to sell my house at a higher price than I expected, and on the very first day it was listed, it sold for full asking price. Was that luck or a sign from God? Who knows? But ready or not, I had better start packing. Moving back to catch a full Las Vegas summer wasn't ideal, but what are ya gonna do?

Karen was right; Boulder is a laid-back, safe town that doesn't care much if people are different, but the truth is, as long as you have a safe, loving, and supportive community of friends around you and you can live openly and honestly, any place is home. When I moved away from Boulder that last time, it wasn't because of a job or finances; I left because I was done. I left on my terms and with complete closure. Colorado will always hold a special place in my life, and I will continue to cherish my old and new friends from there, but I can leave it as a happy memory and not something to chase anymore. Leaving the past in the past and being excited and hopeful for my future in Las Vegas was priceless and freeing.

CHAPTER 12

WHAT'S MISSING?

"The only person you are destined to become is the person you decide to be."

— Ralph Waldo Emerson

Transition is a funny thing. I spent so much time actively waiting and searching for the changes I desired that I kind of missed when they happened. That probably sounds strange. How could I miss morphing from a female to a guy? Well, it's more like I focused all of my attention on a few details like facial hair, voice changes, etc., so I didn't see the whole picture was changing. It didn't happen overnight, but somehow, things fell into line, the girl disappeared, and only a man remained. No longer did anyone call me "Ma'am" on the phone or in person; I was always referred to as "Sir" or some other manly nickname like "Buddy, Bro, Champ"—you get the idea. I don't know the day, month, or year that happened; it just felt like I melted into manhood. It was no longer this awkward elephant in the room, where I was transitioning right in front of everyone and not allowing anyone to mention it. It felt like I had done a complete 180 in a short amount of time.

As time continues to pass, my old identity seems like a distant memory, much like a bad dream. I no longer flinch or turn my head when someone yells my old name in a crowd, because I know it's no longer directed at me. And when I hear that name, it doesn't even register anymore that it used to belong to me. My life has changed so much in big and small ways, and in ways I never thought would be possible.

Physically, of course, I look totally different, yet if you see photos of my past and present day, side-by-side, the two people resemble each other as if they were siblings, but you would never know they were the same person. It seems so foreign to think back about being in a girl's body and being perceived as one. At times, I'm even shocked when I see old photos because the man I see in the mirror now makes far more sense. Even other people have said the same thing and agree that Jeremy is a much better fit.

I finally see those sought after changes every single day. I have a beard now, not the Grizzly Adams' type I had envisioned, but enough that it's mostly noticeable. My hands have changed so much in the last year or so; even though they are still small, they don't resemble girls' hands anymore, which actually surprised me because that change came about only recently. Up until then, I thought having feminine-looking hands was my curse. My skin is rougher, and having wrinkles looks way better as a guy. So the many facial characteristics that I loathed about myself before, now are just me, and I'm fine with them. And thanks to a lot of exercise and a trainer, my body is definitely a dude's. Testosterone is fantastic! As the puzzle pieces started to fit, I began to see the man hiding inside, now staring back at me.

Yet with all that positive change, I'm still feeling incomplete. I look and feel like a man, and that's the identity the world sees as well, but some things are still very disjointed for me. The dysphoria of not having my body look complete in the way I want it to can be very difficult for me. Every time I catch a glimpse of myself in the mirror or in photos, I'm so pleased that I am just a regular guy, but I cringe anytime I have to take my pants off. And the feeling of incompleteness goes well beyond what I don't have in my pants. My body dysphoria, in general, spills over to so many aspects of my life—places I didn't think it would or areas that I thought would get better once I transitioned, like deep friendships and dating.

I had it in my mind that once I was fully a man, life would open up. I would feel complete and dating opportunities would get better because I would be seen as the man who had always been hidden inside. I had always been attracted to straight women, but I didn't always act on it, or I was turned down because they saw my female outward appearance and weren't interested in being in a same-sex relationship. Now that my true identity is on the outside, nothing should stop me, right? Well, I stop me. I get in my own way, and because of my body dysphoria, I assume that women won't want to date a guy like me. The problem isn't with the women; the problem is with me. I still scrutinize over myself and focus more on what I don't have instead of all that I do have. I hone in on the fact that without my clothes on, I look just like a Ken doll, but what I'm forgetting is that even a G.I. Joe action figure doesn't have a dick and he's a manly man.

As I get used to the idea of loving myself, I'm starting to see that people genuinely like/love me too, just for the man I am, but I get in my way and make my body and being transgender a much bigger deal than necessary. My insecurities push women away. I either come off as not being interested in them or I get thrown into the friend zone immediately. When, in fact, what is happening is that I'm afraid to let someone in and I fear rejection because I am not a "complete" man. That may seem strange to many, and I know I have missed many opportunities to date wonderful women, who may have given me a fair chance. I have transferred my lack of fully accepting myself onto others, and I have made being lonely and single a self-fulfilling prophecy. Until I can get a better handle on my dysphoria, I can't guarantee that I won't continue to hide. Every once in awhile, I have a moment of clarity and think, "So what if I don't have a 'normal' penis? Not all women find sex with men comfortable, and there are so many prosthetics and options out there, so I could be any size she wanted. And if we were ever having a fight, and I was kicked to the couch, she could keep the prosthetic in the room with her and still be satisfied." Not a bad deal ladies—just saying. I just need to embrace that kind of thinking all the time.

As a way to help dissolve my body dysphoria, my number one goal is to make enough money so I can have a metoidioplasty procedure, more commonly referred to as "bottom surgery." A metoidioplasty is a surgery some trans guys opt for instead of a phalloplasty (creation of a full-size penis) because a) it's less money, b) you can stand up to urinate, and c) you will retain all sexual sensation. I'll go into more detail about the different surgeries in Chapter 14, but for now, I'll just say that not all trans guys have body dysphoria and some never opt for surgery, but I'm not one of those guys, so bottom surgery weighs heavily on my mind to the point that I have already scheduled a surgery date.

After a ton of research and phone consultations, I chose to schedule my bottom surgery with Dr. Curtis Crane. Dr. Crane joined Dr. Brownstein's practice in San Francisco a couple of years ago, and since I had had my chest surgery with Dr. Brownstein, with fantastic results, I was definitely excited to speak with Dr. Crane. I saw photos of his patient results and read testimonials online, and I was impressed with his surgical background, so I scheduled a consultation. After speaking with Dr. Crane on the phone for about forty-five minutes, I was sold. This was my guy. I sent off my deposit and had a surgery date on the calendar in 2013. The next task was to save a bunch of money. I'll go into the financial details later, but I needed to find about $40,000. I tried all different ways to come up with the money, and at times I almost had enough, but then something always came up, so that money had to be allocated toward my mortgage, eating, and other necessities. Like most trans guys, paying for surgery is the number one obstacle. My health insurance at the time wouldn't pay for any part of the surgery because it wasn't "necessary" and was deemed elective and cosmetic. Perfect. And now that I don't have health insurance anymore, it's obvious that it all has to be paid out-of-pocket.

A couple of times now, I have had to reschedule and push the date further and further out. Fortunately, I have chosen a surgeon who understands this and allows me to move the dates without losing my deposit. Each time I have had to call to reschedule was more difficult than the time before. The last time I called was too much for me and I was devastated. The woman on the phone was so sweet and understanding and reassured me that it would happen for me one day and to remember one thing—my having to cancel now opened up a surgery date for another trans guy on the waiting list to have his dream come true. My day will come as well. In time, I was able to understand what she said, but in that moment, I only cared about myself. After I hung up, I broke down crying. This surgery is necessary for me, and I don't care what an insurance company, specialist, or anyone else says, having bottom surgery and seeing male genitalia when I pull my pants down is crucial to my self-image and self-esteem. It is the one thing that prevents me from feeling complete and seeing myself as a whole man.

I know tons of trans guys don't feel this way, and lots of them are married or in serious, long-term relationships. For many, it's not a major issue, and I'm jealous of those guys. I really wish I felt differently and could accept myself "as is," but for me, and me alone, this is a consuming and crippling issue. It also doesn't help when a complete stranger finds out that I'm transgender and flat out asks me what I have in my pants; yes, that has happened more than once. Not only is that rude; it's like a knife in my heart.

I truly believe that not having "correct" genitalia (to me) is the only reason why I am still single and don't even try to date. I make up a bunch of reasons or excuses to keep women away, and I even emotionally will "go after" unavailable women so I won't feel rejected. When I say "unavailable," I'm not referring to married women or those in relationships, but rather, women who are not looking to date anyone or are not interested in anything other than a friendship with me. I will pick amazing, beautiful women and almost obsess over them, but I know it will never amount to anything. The longer my internal relationship with such women continues, the tougher it is not to fall for them, and then I am upset that it didn't work out or they don't feel the same way because they're already unavailable. The real problem with doing things this way is that I still manage to get hurt, except I do it to myself. Yes, I know that's messed up, but until writing this book, I didn't actually realize that was what I was doing. Instead, I kept thinking, "Why does this keep happening? Why is every woman I'm interested in unavailable? How come I'm tossed into the friend zone with these women, who seem perfect for me?" Well, it keeps happening because I make it so.

I'm in control of finding these women, who never want anything besides a friendship in the first place, and are just good, decent, supportive friends to me, until I mess it up by coming on too strong or squash the friendship because they don't love me back in the same way. All the while, they don't have a clue that any of this is going on. And sometimes, I actually come across an available woman, but I still end up in the friend zone because when an attraction is mutual, I freak out and ruin it before anything can happen—before I either have to disclose my secret or have to take my pants off. Again, I create a self-fulfilling prophecy that no one will want to date me. I make up excuses for why I don't want to date certain "available" women also, such as, "I'm waiting for the one," "She's too tall," or "She's too this or that," but again, the problem is not with her; it's with me.

Even though I've only dated women, my past experiences have

been from a female perspective. All the qualities that women look for in same-sex relationships aren't necessarily the same ones that a straight woman may be looking for in a man. Or maybe they are, but she isn't used to getting them. I'm used to interacting with women as friends and being overly attentive and nurturing. I don't act like the typical guy who's trying to get a woman into bed. I really like to get to know her, listen for small details and cues, and make a woman feel special and appreciated. I even flat out say that's what I like, which tends to make women uncomfortable. I manage to confuse the heck out of women because my intentions are not clear. To be honest, I'm not entirely sure either. I've heard one too many times from women, "You are so nice," "You're not like most men," "You're so sweet…but...." I'm not about to change how I treat women; I just have to believe that there is a woman out there who will want the qualities I have to offer and can see past my perception of a "complete" man.

Will having surgery fix all of this mess? I don't know, but one thing's for sure—feeling and looking like the man I envision will give me way more confidence, which in turn will translate as someone worth getting to know and dating. For now, any rejection I get, whether actual or perceived, is taken by me as "She doesn't want to be with trans guy," when, in fact, the rejection could be simply "She's just not into me as a person," which is just a fact of dating. My guy friends tell me that getting shot down by women is just a rite of passage. Being alone isn't as bad as I may be making it out to be, though. It has given me the time and determination to write this book and make some healthy adjustments to my thinking, and since I'm easily distracted, maybe being single was the only way I would finish it. It all comes down to wanting to feel whole, complete, and to present myself to the world (and to myself) as a man in every way possible. I know that appearance is not what makes a true man and that not having a fully functioning penis doesn't make me less of one either; it's about my character. However, coming to terms with that realization is part of my journey.

So with all that dysphoria chatter floating around in my head, and feeling lonely that I haven't found Mrs. Right or someone to share my home and life with, having to cancel yet another surgery date was painful and I didn't handle it the best way possible. A few days before I had to make that dreaded call, I had received a flyer in the mail from a local Jeep dealership in Colorado, and for some reason, I had saved it on my kitchen counter. Once I rescheduled my surgery date to yet another year away and dried my tears, I got mad. I was frustrated and feeling less than, and that's when I saw that flyer on my counter. I had this crazy idea that I should go get a bad ass Jeep to look cool and manlier, like that would make everything better. Mind you, there was nothing wrong with my current vehicle; in fact, it was only about a year old, but on numerous occasions, I had been teased that I was driving a chick's car, and of course, the people teasing me were just kidding and didn't have a clue about my past, so they had no idea how deep that went. I pretended it didn't bother me, but on that day, I needed to prove I was a man and that I drove a man's car.

I had already planned to hit Home Depot that day to buy a lawn rake, so I thought, "Why not stop into the Jeep dealership while I'm out? What the hell, right?" The flyer was one of those with a plastic key stuck to it, where you bring it in to see whether you won a car or other prizes. It clearly stated that everyone's a winner, so it was definitely a win-win situation. "Who knows?" I thought. "Maybe I'll win a car and can turn around and sell it for surgery money?" After buying my rake, I pulled into the dealership and presented one of the salesman with my flyer. He checked the key and scratch off code, and in fact, I was a winner. I was now the proud owner of two shiny $1.00 coins. Not exactly what I was hoping for. The sales guy handed me my big prize, thanked me for coming in, and walked away. What? No sales pitch? I was stunned and taken aback that he left me standing there in the middle of the showroom.

I played it cool and walked around, checking out the different cars, and then I spotted the Jeep Wrangler Unlimited, the one with four doors. It was awesome. I caught the eye of the same sales guy and asked whether I could sit in it. Of course, I could; it was the showroom, but I wanted to get this guy's attention to see whether he would try to "sell" me something. I always say that I hate haggling at a car dealership, but in all honesty, it's kind of a rush. I wanted that annoying car salesman hard sale. He moseyed on over and made casual chitchat about the Jeep, nothing overbearing, which honestly just pissed me off. I came in ready to haggle and got nothing. I thought, "I'll show this joker who's boss; I'll just buy the damn thing!" That's what happens when I don't deal with my emotions properly. It costs me.

So we went for a test drive in a sweet-looking, all black Jeep Wrangler Unlimited. I felt big, powerful, and manly behind the wheel, even though I would have to have running boards installed just so I could actually get in it. I was so caught up in that stupid moment that I didn't notice that the Jeep didn't fit me well and didn't drive the way I had expected. Because of my short stature, it was difficult to reach the gas pedal comfortably, but somehow, I missed that detail since my head was up my own ass. We got back from the test drive, I signed the papers, handed over my trade-in, loaded up my new rake, and headed home. Life was good. I lied to my friends that I had bought the Jeep because my old car didn't handle the Colorado snow well and my monthly payments were exactly the same. Both were untrue.

Over the next few weeks, I noticed I couldn't get comfortable while driving and my right knee started to hurt. I couldn't get the seat to move up close enough, so my right leg never rested on the ground while I was driving; it basically hovered above the floorboard with just my toes hitting the gas pedal. This meant my leg and hip muscles stayed contracted the entire time I was behind the wheel. Then the pain started and I began to limp. Not the cool swagger type of limp, but more like an old guy in need of a hip replacement. It got so bad that I didn't even want to drive anymore, so I had another great idea to buy pedal extenders. I swear I buy more crap online that's supposed to make my life better, instead of being realistic and making better choices upfront. But, anyway, I bought the extenders, installed them, which wasn't as easy as the directions claimed, and drove with them for a few days. They were awkward and didn't help that much, mostly because I couldn't get the placement just right.

One early morning, I jumped in the Jeep that was parked in my garage. I put my foot on the brake extender, popped it into reverse, and instantly realized I had my foot mostly on the gas and a little bit on the brake. Apparently, I had installed the two extenders too close to each other. With most of my weight on the gas pedal, when I put it into reverse, the Jeep began to shake, the engine revved, and I shot out of my garage at warp speed. I literally laid rubber in my garage. Thankfully, I had put the garage door up or I would've smashed right through the new doors I had installed a few months earlier. I was scared shitless. I came to a screeching halt at the end of my driveway and an exhaust cloud billowed out of the garage. I'm so glad it was still dark outside and none of my neighbors were up to see the spectacle. My heart was in my throat and my hands were shaking, but I had to get to work, so I drove super slow and kept thinking the entire day, "Oh, crap, I'm going to have to drive home." Needless to say, I took the pedal extenders off that night and sent them back. Leg and hip pain were better than crashing.

I did end up taking the Wrangler back to the dealership to explain what was going on. I have to say that Prestige Chrysler Jeep in Longmont, Colorado, was awesome. The salesman let me return the vehicle and downsize to a smaller Jeep Patriot. I didn't look as cool and felt more like I should be driving kids to soccer, but my limp went away. Moral of the story: Don't buy shit when you're upset. I felt badly about myself, and in a rash decision, thought that a big fancy Jeep, something material, would make me feel better. I know I was just compensating for not feeling man enough, which, in hindsight, is kind of a rite of passage as well. I think we've all seen that guy driving down the road in his compensation vehicle.

Now one would hope that after a costly lesson like the Jeep experience, I would realize I was overcompensating for feeling incomplete, but sadly no. I was still searching for ways to make myself feel better, more adequate. While I regret buying the Jeep because it only added a bigger car payment, I don't regret the next decision I made. Even though I couldn't afford to have surgery, I had saved up some money and decided to use a bit of it to have a facial hair transplant. That is exactly what it sounds like; hair from the back of the head is transplanted onto the face.

I had always wanted a full mustache and beard; facial hair that I could shave and mold into a goatee, muttonchops, anything I could imagine, and it would be glorious. Unfortunately, I took after most men in my family and couldn't grow a beard to save my life. Again, I was disappointed with myself and focused on the things I didn't have. I could grow a mustache, but my beard was very patchy and thin, and my chin was as bare as a baby's butt. Not a hair in sight. I tried Rogaine, even though it clearly says on the box not to put the product on your face. The only thing it did was burn and cause acne—perfect. That's probably why there's a warning on the box. I would color the fuzz I did have, hoping it would help and make the hair more noticeable, but it just brought more attention to the hot mess I was trying to grow on my face.

So I dipped into my savings and scheduled a beard transplant. I didn't want anyone to know I was planning this, and for those who didn't know I was transgender, I lied and said I had a connection back in Las Vegas to get this done for free in exchange for helping with a marketing campaign for a hair restoration company. My thinking was, "If I tell people it's free, they won't give me grief for wasting my money on something that crazy, or interrogate me as to why I would even want to have the procedure done." I'm sorry to those I lied to, but I panicked and didn't know what to say or do. The procedure was scheduled for a few days before Thanksgiving of 2013. I told Gerald and Belinda at the last minute, but overall, I kept it pretty much on the down low.

It was an outpatient procedure where the surgeon took a section of hair and scalp from the back of my head just like with any other hair transplant and implanted the hairs and follicles onto my face, one by one. The numbing process was rough since the medicine had to be injected all over my face, but once my head and face were completely numb, it wasn't that bad. The surgeon literally made tiny incisions all over my face where the hairs would be implanted; somewhere around 1,500 grafts were done. It was definitely a long day. Once the hairs were implanted on my face and my scalp was sewn up with twenty-one stitches, I headed back home in the cab to heal up over the next week.

I looked pretty rough, and my face was extremely swollen with tiny scabs all over my cheeks and chin. The back of my head felt like I'd been kicked by a horse, and because my cheeks and new grafts couldn't touch the pillow at night, I had to lie on the healing incision. My original thought was, "Take a week off of work, and by the time I go back, I should be healed enough that it won't be that noticeable." Not sure what I was thinking, but after one week, I was not completely healed and it was very noticeable. Thankfully, I was a good liar, and everyone at work bought the story that I had the procedure done for free and thought I was a great friend to help out someone else's business. Not sure how I came up with that story, but it seemed plausible and was a way I could talk about the procedure without talking about myself. I definitely had to say something once I got back to work because you couldn't help but stare at my face. So much for wanting to blend in.

For the longest time, I looked the same as I did before the surgery, and I kept bugging the guy at the hair clinic, thinking that the grafts didn't take. I worried that I would be stuck with a bald chin, patchy hair on my cheeks, and a five-inch scar across the back of my head. I knew the transplanted hairs would fall out because the follicles were being implanted, but I was expecting the hair to grow much faster. But just as the clinic director and numerous Google searches claimed, in time hair started to grow. It's not perfect, but at least there's something there. What's weird is that the hair is darker since it's from the back of my head and softer, not like true facial hair, so as it grows longer it actually blows in the wind and tickles. But I'm super stoked and very happy that I did it.

For many people reading this, it may seem so foreign that I would pay money just to have some facial hair because a lot of guys can't grow a full beard, but for me, that hair is directly connected to my self-image, my confidence, and my manhood. I will admit that a constant concern of mine is being mistaken for a female, even today. It doesn't happen anymore, but I remember when it did early on, and I don't ever want to be mistaken again. Facial hair is like my security blanket or my insurance policy, if you will. And even though I may not have the most attractive beard and some may think I should shave it off, now you know why it means so much to me and why it is necessary for my wellbeing.

CHAPTER 13

COMING FULL CIRCLE

"You gain strength, courage, and confidence by every experience in which you really stop to look fear in the face. You must do the thing which you think you cannot do."

— Eleanor Roosevelt

S o as my life started to fall into place, and I began to feel much more complete, I was beginning to hit my stride. I was becoming more comfortable with myself, but I would soon be put to the test.

In April, 2014, my uncle Jim passed away after battling a type of blood cancer called myelodysplastic syndrome (MDS). My uncle was my dad's only sibling; they were business partners, and we lived two doors down from my uncle's family when I was growing up. It felt like I had two families when I was younger, and most people thought I belonged to my aunt and uncle because I looked like my cousins, which paid off nicely when I was able to use my cousin Sue's ID before I turned twenty-one. There weren't a lot of us Wallaces in our small hometown, but everyone knew us since my dad and uncle owned the local grocery store. Being around extended family growing up was great, and I definitely took it for granted that my family would always be around. Over the years as we all scattered to other states, I didn't do a great job of staying in close contact with my aunt, uncle, and cousins, like I had wanted to, but again thanks to Facebook, it felt like we were still in each other's lives. They all knew about my transition from the get-go, as I mentioned earlier, and they were more than supportive.

So when I got the call that Uncle Jim wasn't going to make it more than a few more days, I knew I had to go back home to Michigan. This would be the first time I had been back to my hometown as Jeremy. At first, I wasn't nervous at all to make the trip because it was important for me to be there for my family, for my dad, and to have a chance to say goodbye. My dad and sister flew in from Florida and made it in time to see my uncle while he was still conscious enough to know that they were there, and I am so happy that my dad was able to have that moment. Unfortunately, because of my mom's health, she was unable to make the trip.

By the time I flew in the following day, Uncle Jim had slipped into a coma. I was able to spend a few moments alone with him to tell him that I loved him, thank him for loving me, and say goodbye. Even if he didn't appear to hear me, I know he did. I held his hand and prayed for his peaceful passing. Having that time with him will forever mean the world to me.

Uncle Jim hung on until the early hours of the next morning, probably because there were so many people crammed in his room, all telling stories and reminiscing, and he always loved a full house. Almost all of the stories brought laughter to the group, which he always enjoyed, so I'm sure it was hard for him to go. He fought so hard until peace and heaven called him home.

Before Uncle Jim passed, a small group of us were in the family lounge area, which the Wallace clan basically overtook, telling stories, sharing memories, and discussing his final wishes. It was a bit awkward to be making funeral plans before he passed, but it had to be done. Everyone felt helpless, like we were just passing time, waiting for the inevitable. It was at this time that all of my career hopping and dabbling finally paid off since I was actually able to do something in this helpless moment. From my brief time in mortuary school, I could actually help advise and guide my aunt. Funeral arrangements are extremely difficult, not because of the process or the paperwork, but because everyone's emotions are so raw. Decisions had to be made rather quickly without a lot of time to sit back and digest what was really happening. Add grief and sadness to trying to plan the perfect tribute to someone you love and don't want to let go of, and it all makes for an overwhelming experience. Being able to step in and ease that moment made me feel like I had something to contribute. I think my aunt and cousins were relieved not to have to navigate this on their own.

As we were discussing details like which funeral home to use and the logistics of what the services would look like, my aunt said she really wanted someone to speak at the memorial. The room became silent; everyone looked around at each other. Now to make a group of Wallaces become silent is a feat unto itself. Aunt Judy stated emphatically that it wasn't going to be her, and each of my cousins echoed the same sentiment, as well as my dad. Everyone sat there waiting for someone to come up with an idea or suggestion. My heart began to race because I knew what I needed to do. I volunteered to speak at the memorial. I could hardly believe the words that came out of my mouth when I said I would do it, and all the family looked at me with a combination of surprise at my offer and relief that they didn't have to.

Now that the offer was said out loud, a bit of panic set in. Since I worry about everything, did I really think that volunteering to speak at a funeral in front of my hometown wouldn't clamp my sphincter tight as a drum? I knew I could do it and it was an honor, but I also remembered my aunt saying that she expected about 250 people to be in attendance. We were from a very small town, so that number would include a lot of the townsfolk—people who used to know me as Jenny, but probably didn't know about my transition. Holy shit! So I had to address what I perceived as the elephant in the room and ask whether everyone was really okay with me speaking. I said that, when I start talking, people will catch on quickly and will figure out who I am and who I used to be. My dad only had two kids, so it would be really easy to figure out. My concern was that I would be a distraction from why we were all together, that I would take the focus off celebrating my uncle.

Without hesitation or skipping a beat, my aunt, in a tone that I equate with a verbal slap in the face, said, "What the hell do you care?" Just like that. I was stunned and went silent. My cousins jumped right in with a resounding, "Yeah, who cares?" I don't ever recall being verbally spanked that hard and being put in my place, and I didn't know whether I should cry, be angry, or laugh. That simple question changed my life. I felt like I had been punched in the stomach by reason and clarity. Why *did* I care? And in that moment, I no longer did. I couldn't have asked for or dreamed of a better reaction from my family, and I truly realized I had been making my transition too big of a deal for way too long. I had been hiding behind it and not living authentically. I had been using my trans status as an excuse and as a crutch to avoid living up to my full potential. So that was that. I would be speaking at the memorial service, not just for myself, but also for everyone in my family who could not.

The next few days after my uncle passed were hectic as we got the funeral plans hammered out, and each night when we got back to our hotel, I would work on my speech. I wrote draft after draft, and the night usually ended with me crumpling up the paper and tossing it out. How in the world do you capture someone's essence?

I had so many memories and stories swirling around in my head that I couldn't seem to put anything together. Fortunately, my family is a bunch of storytellers, and I was able to absorb some great tales from others that I could include into my speech. It wasn't until the night before the memorial that I was able to write something that embodied my uncle's spirit, his zest for family and life, and I managed to put it all together in a way that I hoped the crowd would enjoy. My uncle loved to laugh and never seemed to mind being the reason for the laughter, and I think I captured that pretty well.

As a family, we made it through the visitation and small private graveside funeral the day before the big memorial. I'm pretty sure I was a pain in the funeral director's butt since I knew just enough about the funeral industry to keep him on his toes and make him nervous. I didn't mean to be a pain, but I demanded that my uncle and his family get the best customer service possible and be treated with the utmost respect.

The only thing left was the large memorial service, and of course, I was very nervous. Fortunately, you can't see sweat through a black suit. My aunt quietly told me she was proud of me for speaking, and if I got too nervous, just to look up and give the speech to her and my cousins in the front row. That's who I was there for anyway. Over the last week, I had had a chance to connect with quite a few people I hadn't seen in years, if not decades, many of whom had flown in or driven long distances to pay their respects and support the Wallace family. My aunt and cousins, unknown to me, had been talking to others about me and my transition from the very beginning. So many people already knew, and they were all genuinely happy to see me and made everything feel normal.

My family hadn't discussed me in a gossipy sort of way, but more of a matter of fact way, just catching people up to what had been going on. They were all proud of me, and keeping my transition and me a secret never occurred to them; I wish it had never occurred to me either. My nervousness over feeling exposed and vulnerable faded each time a familiar face would show up at my aunt's house. And time and time again, people reached out with handshakes and hugs like I had been Jeremy to them all along, just wanting to know how I had been and glad to see me happy at last. I had grossly underestimated my family, friends, and past acquaintances, and I was truly humbled. I reconnected with so much of my past, and by doing so, I thought my heart would explode with joy. It wasn't awkward or weird; it just felt normal and right. I could be myself completely, and it was amazing.

By the time I stood up to speak at the memorial, my only nerves were about public speaking and whether my speech would suck. My speech went better than I could have hoped for; there was laughter at the right moments, and I was told I delivered it with confidence, like I was a natural in front of a crowd. I have to say I was proud of myself too and happy that I was able to share memories of my uncle with everyone. I didn't blatantly "come out" in the speech, but everyone there could figure it out from my referencing who my dad was and from all of the stories. Like I said, it was a small town where everyone knew our name. After I sat back down, I was completely at ease and relieved. I knew that I would see and mingle with the crowd once we went to the lunch venue, but I no longer cared what anyone thought of me. I was there to pay tribute to my uncle and to support and spend time with my family. Nothing else mattered.

At the lunch, I was taken aback and amazed by the outpouring of accolades I received, mostly about my speech; it was appreciated and enjoyed, and I'm not going to lie, that was just the ego boost I needed, and it felt great. One couple, whom I had known all my years growing up and whose son I had played high school hockey with, came up to me just to reintroduce themselves and to let me know they were proud of me. They said they knew that transitioning took courage, and I finally looked happy. It sounds really strange to say, but my uncle's funeral was an amazing, life-changing event for me. I wish it could have happened without losing him, but I know that God works in very mysterious ways and that my uncle was right there by my side the entire time. He gave me a gift I will forever be grateful for.

The rest of that afternoon, I shook hands, gave and received a ton of hugs, and most of all, made new "old" friends. Letting my guard down, taking a risk, and letting my true self be seen opened up my life. I'm so blessed to have had this experience all while being surrounded by my already supportive family.

That night at the hotel, which was my last night in Michigan, my dad and I sat up late reminiscing and chatting about life. I expressed that I didn't know which direction to go in anymore and that I was unhappy in Colorado, lonely, and felt stuck. Now my dad usually takes the role of devil's advocate, whether solicited or not, but this time was different. He really listened and asked me what I wanted to do, not what I thought I should do. He agreed that if I wasn't happy in Boulder, I should move. He said, "Go back to where you have a large group of friends," and "Home isn't a geographical place; it's where you are happy. Any place can be home if you have the right support." I was already thinking of moving back to Las Vegas, but I didn't have any job prospects.

My dad finally said out loud what I had been feeling which was, "You seem to be floundering, bouncing around from job to job, none of which seem to fit you; what do you really want to do?" Huh? Something seemed to change when "really" was added to that question. I thought of so many things I should say, but then remembered a phrase I had heard before, "Don't *should* on yourself." So I answered with the truth for once. I wanted to finish writing my story and travel around speaking to groups, bringing awareness to being transgender, all while providing an educational and entertaining experience. There, I had said it out loud and I wanted a career living out loud, sharing my journey, and for once I was no longer afraid.

I sat and waited for the negativity—the reasons why I shouldn't rely on that as a career—and being asked what was my backup plan to support myself. But that never came. Instead, my dad smiled and said, "Then I think you should do that." Seriously? Who was this guy? He thought selling my house and taking a few months to finish my book and get things rolling was a great idea. But he had seen me step up, face my fears and hometown, speak eloquently during a very difficult time, and handle it all like a man. He knew I was ready, and for once, so did I. I would have thought it far-fetched that a trip back to my childhood town could be the catalyst to embracing myself fully as a man, but in actuality, that is exactly what happened. I can honestly say that I am not the same person after that week in Michigan. My family and I lost a great and important person, but through his passing, Uncle Jim gave us all so much more. I thank Uncle Jim for bringing my future to life. I've already mentioned that I sold my house in Colorado and moved back to Las Vegas just in time to catch the long hot summer. It was also around that time that I got in touch with my writing and speaking coach Patrick and caught him up to speed on my book and myself. So with all that taken care of and a new lease on life, I embarked on a journey of completing this book. I'm sure it appeared to outsiders that I was just hanging out and wasting time, but they didn't know I was writing or realize I was truly serious about this venture. Any snide remarks fell on deaf ears because I was on a mission.

As I was wrapping up the last few chapters, I decided to attend one of Patrick Snow's Best-Seller Publishing Institute conferences. Patrick does these three-day workshops six times a year in different locations, which are attended by his clients and are great networking opportunities; of course, they also offer intensive guidance and information about book writing, publishing, and speaking. I had wanted to go to one earlier, but I was too afraid that I wouldn't be accepted because I was transgender and my story wouldn't be well-received. But now that Patrick knew and was really excited about my story, he reassured me that not only would I be accepted, but I would be embraced. He said not to worry because he had clients from all walks of life and they were amazing people.

So I trusted Patrick and went to the workshop in Seattle. I kept hearing my aunt's voice saying, "What the hell do you care?" over and over. It was a great reminder, and after standing tall in front of my hometown, I knew that being in a room with thirty strangers would be okay. I needed to learn more about the entire book process, and this was the way to do it, not to mention if I were to embark on a speaking career based on my life, I would have to take risks like this.

Oddly enough, as I traveled to Seattle, I wasn't nervous at all. I was excited and ready to tell my story. I got there just in time, and the workshop was off and running. We went around the room and did introductions, which included telling everyone who you were, where you were from, the title and a very brief synopsis of your book, and then something unique about yourself. I sat there and listened to all of my new colleagues, but of course, I was apprehensive to stand up to speak. I am my own worst critic, and I always want everything to be perfect, so of course, I worried that I wouldn't do well. That even sounds stupid to me because how could I not do well? I only had to answer questions about myself, and of course, I knew the answers. So naturally, I was at the table that was the last to go. I realized that everyone was in the same boat, and almost everyone was uncomfortable to get up in front of the group, but everyone did a great job.

When it was my turn to stand up, I remember saying my name and that I was from Las Vegas, but after that, it's a bit fuzzy because this would be the first time I would say out loud the title of my book and what it was about. I could see my hand shaking as I held the microphone, but I managed to tell the group, "My book is titled, *Taking the Scenic Route to Manhood,* and my book is about my journey through the genders since I was born a female. I am transgender." I have no idea whether I said anything else because by now my ears were buzzing, but I do remember telling the group that I couldn't think of anything else that was unique about me. Of course, that got the group laughing.

Once I sat back down at my table, I glanced around at those sitting with me, hoping that they would at least smile and not be freaked out. Turns out I was sitting at the best table in the house, and after those three days, I can honestly call those three women my friends. So the cat was out of the bag and nobody shunned me or freaked out—in fact, most people wanted to talk to me.

The next few days flew by, and I met so many wonderful people, all with amazing stories to tell. On the last day, we were all able to give a ten-minute speech, basically a shortened version of what we would be talking about when someone hired us to give a keynote speech. The night before I jotted down some notes, some key points I wanted to hit, but I wasn't exactly sure what direction I wanted to take. Did I want to tell a funny story or something more serious? But when I actually started the speech, I ended up winging it, somewhat. Somehow, I managed to combine serious with humor, and it went really well. In fact, I received a standing ovation, and when Patrick asked me how it felt to receive a standing O after my very first speech, it took everything I had not to burst into tears. I knew I had not only found my calling and passion, but I was actively pursuing it.

All in all, those three days were so positive and I learned so much. All my anxiety and nervousness about attending was again a waste of time. I only encountered one person who made me feel uncomfortable, but I don't think that was her intention. After I gave my speech on the last day, I had to leave early to get to the airport, and because I was catching a ride with two other women, our leaving at the same time created a kind of distraction, which prompted an unscheduled break. I was glad that happened because it gave me a chance to say goodbye to all of my new friends and make sure we exchanged contact info. For all the nerves I had coming to the conference, I was now sad to leave.

Just as I was making my way to the door, a woman came up to me. She must've been one of the few who only came for the last day because I didn't know or recognize her. She was nice and smiled warmly, but then began to stutter as she said, "So you used to be....and now you're...?" She said this all while keeping the smile, which turned out to be more like an exaggerated squint that people have when they are searching for the right words to ask an inappropriate question. You know, that look that's well on its way to turning into the, "I'm constipated" face. She finally ended that choppy line of questioning by saying, "You've had your breasts cut off, right?" I answered with, "Yes, I've had a double mastectomy with chest reconstruction." Not sure whether I used too many big words in that answer or what, but she seemed both surprised and confused.

And then it came, the squint followed by the dreaded, "Can I ask you something else?" and she glanced down at my pants. I knew exactly what she wanted to know, but I put my hand up in a gesture that conveyed, "Stop," and I politely said, "I'm sorry, but we've never met before, and I don't know you well enough to be discussing that. So no, you can't ask me that and I'm not comfortable answering your question." She started backpedaling and trying to figure out how to make this better; the only thing she could come up with was to thank me for my honesty. An apology would have been nicer, but I truly don't believe that she understood how inappropriate that exchange was. Clearly that was not the answer she was hoping for, but I reassured her that when my book was out, she would have an opportunity to buy it if she really wanted to learn more.

This wasn't the first, nor will it be the last time that someone asks me in a roundabout way what is or isn't in my pants, and unfortunately for anyone who is transgender, that's just a reality. It's hard for me to wrap my head around why that is the number one thing people want to know—and why a complete stranger believes he or she is entitled to know. Asking anyone about what his or her genitalia looks like is inappropriate. Period. It's like going up to a male wounded warrior in a wheelchair, thanking him for his service, and then asking him, "Hey, since you're paralyzed now, does your dick still work?" Would anyone do that? Now to be clear, I am in no way comparing my experience to that of someone in our Armed Forces sacrificing his life. I'm just trying to make a point about how crazy it is to ask anyone such personal questions, especially without there first being any attempt to get to know who you are as a person. Would I have felt different about this woman and her line of questioning had I spent the last three days getting to know her on a personal level? Maybe. It bothered me so much because it felt like she made a beeline for me, only to satisfy her curiosity, and not actually to meet or get to know who I was. My hope is that this was a teachable moment for her and for anyone else who may be reading this.

That moment in no way clouded my experience at the workshop. I left Seattle with pep in my step and eager to get my career underway. Because of that amazing week in Michigan, followed by the workshop in Seattle, I emerged a stronger, more confident man who could stand up for himself and not let the little things get under his skin. I knew my future was just beginning.

CHAPTER 14

THE SIX MILLION DOLLAR TRANSMAN

"The best way to predict the future is to create it."
— Peter Drucker

First of all, don't get your panties or boxers in a bunch; it doesn't cost $6 million to do this work, but as I said in the first chapter, I always related to Steve Austin a bit. However, making the necessary life and physical changes so your body, mind, and soul completely match can be very expensive. And getting your insurance company to help out or pay for surgeries and hormones can be difficult, to say the least. That's assuming you have insurance at all. It is not unheard of for someone to lose his or her job, be denied better positions that include benefits, or not be hired at all, just for being transgender. Discrimination happens; that's just a fact.

Times are changing, although slowly, and we are starting to see more companies and organizations with diversity and inclusion policies that specifically include transgender employees and recruits. And as I have mentioned earlier, some insurance carriers are beginning to cover transgender-related healthcare. Because of the Affordable Health Care Act, being transgender is no longer a pre-existing condition or a reason to deny someone coverage. But just because someone is eligible for health insurance doesn't mean he or she can afford the very high premiums. And if you qualify for Medicaid or Medicare, the same problems arise just as if you had any other insurance; your day-to-day health stuff is covered, but anything trans-related can be excluded. I am definitely not an expert on healthcare, but there are many resources out there to shed more light on this topic, some of which are listed in the Resources section at the end of this book. So suffice it to say, the majority of transgender people have to pay out-of-pocket, which for some is impossible.

So how much does it cost? Well, that's a good question and one that I get often, and the answer varies from person to person. There's a lot more involved than people realize. A lot happens very early in transition, even before family and friends may know that their loved one is transgender. If you recall, I mentioned earlier the World Professional Association for Transgender Health (WPATH) standards of care guidelines and "rules," or hoops you have to jump through just to live a more authentic life. Some of the "guidelines" say that one must live full-time as his or her chosen gender, be in therapy, and be diagnosed as having a Gender Identity Disorder, all before the person can be put on hormones or have surgeries.

Fortunately, not all the guidelines are strictly adhered to anymore, and I don't know of anyone, personally, who wasn't able to start hormones at the early onset of transition, rather than having to wait the year. I couldn't imagine living a full year as Jeremy, without hormone replacement and supporting documentation. I know a lot of guys who have to do that for various reasons, and I think they are very brave. One "rule" that seems to be very strict is that for transgender-identified people to get medically necessary hormones and surgeries/healthcare, they need a therapist letter, or what Transgender & Transsexual Road Map calls a "Ritual Document" (see its website www.tsroadmap.com).

Referring to the therapist letter this way fits well because therapy can be seen as a ritual we have to participate in so we can move forward. But to get that letter, like I did, you have to go to counseling with a legitimate and licensed therapist, which, of course, costs money. Some insurance carriers cover mental health visits, but the therapist you feel comfortable and safe with may not be on your insurance carrier's list, and again, that's assuming one has health insurance. So before transition can really begin, transgender people are already in the red financially.

Once we have that letter, or Golden Ticket, the next task is to find a doctor for hormone therapy. For myself, it wasn't too difficult finding a doctor in my area who was willing to work with trans patients, but my choices were limited. It's not uncommon for trans people to obtain their hormones through other, non-medical sources out of desperation, which is totally understandable, but unsafe. Going that route, you never know what you're getting or the quality of the hormones, and you aren't being monitored by a doctor.

When a doctor is found, office visits are costly and hormones can range from $50 to $100 a vial for injectable testosterone, which lasts about four to six months, depending on dosage, topical creams (which without insurance can be upwards of a few hundred dollars), and testosterone pellets (which are implanted under the skin and can cost $200 to $300 every six months), not including the office visit. That may not seem exorbitantly high for some, but it adds up quickly, and hormone therapy is necessary for many transgender, not to mention, it may be necessary for a lifetime, depending on the person.

As we transgenders really get into our journeys, we have to change our clothing to match. Of course, this can be the fun part, to go out shopping for clothes, shoes, and accessories that express our true gender identity, but it's expensive too. You basically have to replace your entire closet. Thankfully for me, I already wore a lot of typical guys clothes, so I didn't have to start from scratch, but I had a ton of girl stuff I needed to get rid of. It was liberating to pack up anything that was remotely girly and drop it off at Goodwill, never looking back. It made me feel manly to buy a suit, especially when I bought it at the Men's Warehouse. How could I go wrong when the store said, "Men's" on the sign out front?

While the counseling, hormones, and clothing add up financially, they are, of course, well worth it. And for some guys, that's enough, but for myself, the next necessary step was surgery. That's where it gets very expensive and unobtainable for many. For the layperson, the term surgery means sex change operations, but that's not exactly accurate. There are so many surgical procedures for female-to-male (FTM) and male-to-female (MTF) that it's almost an insult to call them all a "sex change." For those transitioning FTM, the options run the spectrum from top surgery, having breasts removed, to bottom surgery, which could mean having a hysterectomy, metoidioplasty, or phalloplasty. (I'll explain all those in a minute.) Which surgery to have is a very personal decision, and any of the options, from not having any surgery at all to having multiple, is the right choice. For MTF, in addition to breast augmentation, vaginoplasty, or removing the penis and creating a vagina, there are facial feminization surgeries and hair transplant procedures to name a few. I only have experience with transitioning from female-to-male, so I'm sure there are other MTF procedures that I am not aware of, but all in all, there are many options for all transgender people, all of which are medically necessary for some.

So what are some of these FTM surgeries? Having breasts removed is pretty self-explanatory. No guy wants to have boobs, even those who love to play with 'em don't want them on their own chests. To have breasts removed obviously requires a surgeon who is experienced and skilled in the procedure and who can sculpt the end result into a masculine chest. If you are very small-breasted, the option may be a "keyhole" procedure, where an incision is made around the nipple area and liposuction is used to remove the breast tissue. This procedure minimizes the scar to just around the outside of the areola, and typically, it leaves the nerve sensation intact. All trans guys want this option for obvious reasons, but in actuality, a ton of guys are not candidates for the keyhole procedure because their breasts are too large, meaning they are bigger than a small A cup, or the breast tissue sags too much.

For me, I wasn't large-chested by any means, but big enough that I had to have the double incision procedure or full mastectomy with chest reconstruction. What that entails is two incisions below each breast, the breast tissue removed, and the skin from the top of the breast is pulled down flat and stitched to the incision. The excess skin is tossed out. The nipples are also removed and grafted back on in the correct position. This procedure resulted, for me, in not having sensation in my nipples.

Naturally, the recovery time is far greater with a double mastectomy, and the option is more costly. I have found chest surgery ranges anywhere from $5,000 to $8,000, depending on the surgeon, procedure, pre-op tests, and fees. My best advice is to pick a surgeon based on desired results either from pictures, videos, or talking with another trans guy, and not based on price alone. You get what you pay for, and if the look you want costs a bit more, it's worth every penny. This is your chance to bring a dream to reality, so you want to make sure you love the results.

Also, remember there are additional costs like travel, accommodations, and meals that need to be figured in too if the surgeon is not close by. All said and done, my top surgery came in around $10,000, which included the surgery, pre-op tests, hotel, meals, and round trip airfare from Las Vegas to San Francisco. Not cheap for sure, but thanks to my parents, I was able to pull this off.

Now bottom surgery is a different story. A lot of trans guys only opt for hormones and chest surgery and are very happy. While it's true that it is no one's business what anyone has or doesn't have in his pants, in my case, my gender dysphoria is too great, so not a day goes by that I don't agonize over having what I feel is the wrong genitalia. This has stunted my happiness, but I know I will make it happen one day. There are different options for bottom surgery like a pre-meta or clitoral release, where the surrounding skin of the clitoris is removed and the ligament is released from the pubic bone. That allows that little guy to stand up when excited. Definitely an oversimplification, but you get the idea. With a release, you won't be able to stand up to pee, but it's still an option if one can't afford a full metoidioplasty or wants to do things in stages. This option ranges from $5,000 to $20,000, depending on the surgeon, pre-op stuff, and whether or not other procedures are done at the same time, like a hysterectomy or oophorectomy, which is the removal of the uterus and ovaries.

A full metoidioplasty with urethral lengthening, which is the option I have chosen, releases the clitoris as well, but the urethra is lengthened and repositioned so that urine will be expelled from the end instead of underneath, which makes it possible to stand up to pee. At the same time, a hysterectomy and oophorectomy can be performed as well, and then the vaginal opening is surgically closed. Having the uterus and ovaries removed takes away the risks of uterine, ovarian, and cervical cancers, as well as never having to experience another humiliating and embarrassing pelvic exam. So removing that crap, since I have no desire to use it, is not only good for my physical health, but my mental wellbeing too. Not only can you stand up to pee like other guys, but the end result looks like a small penis.

At this point, a scrotoplasty can be done, which basically is surgically creating balls. The labia skin is made into a scrotum, and testicular implants can be put in, but they are not necessary. It seems kind of weird to pay good money to have balls since they're kinda gross looking, but not having them is even weirder. Rarely is the small phallus large enough for sex, but as long as I don't see a female body staring back at me in the mirror, it's great! A full metoidioplasty can range from $10,000 to $60,000 and better, depending on the factors I mentioned above and whether or not the uterus and ovaries are removed and a scrotoplasty is performed.

Some guys choose to go even a step further and have a surgery called a phalloplasty. Yes, that is exactly what you think it is—surgically creating a full-size penis. This is a pretty complex surgery for trans guys; it is very expensive, has more complications, and the end results are not exactly what we had hoped for. The phallus is created with skin taken from the forearm, back, or thigh, as well as the nerves, and after about nine months or so of healing time, a penile implant can be put in so an erection can be achieved. The same type of implant is used in guys with erectile dysfunction. The number one criticism of this surgery is that sexual sensation, if any remains, is decreased, and the penis doesn't really look realistic, nor does it function like a cis male's penis. A lot of progress is being made in phalloplasty surgery, but for me personally, it's just not there yet. I've always thought, "How cool would it be for a trans woman who desperately wants to get rid of a penis to be able to donate it to a trans guy?" If only it worked like that, but sadly, it doesn't. Needless to say, all bottom surgeries are expensive, but the phalloplasty takes the cake, costing anywhere from $50,000 to $100,000 and beyond.

So how does anyone who is transgender afford these surgeries? Honestly, many can't. Those who do undergo them try anything possible such as help from family and friends, Internet funding sites, insurance, working additional jobs, and just saving every penny that comes in. No matter how, getting the funds can be daunting, stressful, and take years. I think about having bottom surgery all the time, and it affects my daily budget because I'm constantly thinking about how I can make and save the necessary funds, all while still affording my rent and living essentials. Just when I think I am on track, something always comes up, so I've had to push back my surgery date numerous times as I've said. I've never felt like it's not going to happen, even though I have been extremely frustrated that I can't pinpoint the when or how. Obviously, when I owned my own business, I would have been able to save more and have afforded it by now, but apparently, that's not how it's supposed to be.

I'm not sure whether it was a mistake or not, but when my family sold its business, instead of using my share of the money for surgery, I chose to move to Colorado and buy that house. I also made the decision to take some time off and just bum around while living off my savings because I had never had that opportunity before. Was that smart? That depends. It was in that bumming around period that I bounced around from job to job, but I also finally realized my passion and what I wanted to do with my life, which was to write this book and speak to others. So I'd say that realizing my dream and going after it was worth it. I wish I had figured it out a little faster, though. As I've mentioned before, I basically flipped that house and fixed it up enough that when I sold it, I made a profit. I don't care what anyone says; real estate is a great investment, as long as you are patient, put some work into it, and of course, the timing is right. So why am I mentioning my business and house again? At times, I've had the money or most of it for surgery, and it always came from multiple income streams; I just chose to spend it elsewhere or gave up too soon.

To pay for these surgeries is going to take creativity and thinking outside the box, as well as making sure I have a career that will not just pay my living expenses, but afford me to build savings that can be used toward continuing and maintaining my transition. I'm reminded again of Patrick Snow's book, *Creating Your Own Destiny,* and why I picked up the book in the first place. The title alone grabbed my attention and made me realize that if I wanted something badly enough, instead of being defeated, I would just have to figure out a different way to achieve it.

Every single person is capable of becoming the person he or she is meant to be and having the future he or she dreams of. Many may be thinking, "But I don't have a business of my own or a house to sell; I have nothing. What am I supposed to do?" My answer is, "You do whatever it takes; envision yourself being successful and achieving your goals, and then you never take no for an answer." Easier said than done, right? Actually, no. And the reason I can be that confident saying "No" is because for every single transgender person out there, you have to look at what you have already accomplished by just transitioning. You already know how to think outside the box and overcome adversity, all while going against the grain and surviving. We are definitely a resilient group.

For many of us, there is fear and anxiety about coming out as transgender in the workplace; fear that we will lose our jobs, be harassed, or won't even have the chance to get the job. So my challenge to anyone who feels this way is to ask yourself, "Is there any way I can create my own job?" Depending on what line of work you are in or trying to pursue, that may not be possible. But if that's the case, then at least be proactive and do some research on companies that embrace diversity and inclusion, especially companies listed on the Human Rights Campaign's (HRC) Corporate Equality Index. The HRC puts together an index or list of businesses and how they rate in terms of their treatment, advancement, etc. of LGBT employees. According to its website (www.hrc.org), over 300 businesses have earned a top score of 100 percent and have the distinction of "Best Places to Work for LGBT Equality." The cool thing is that the businesses on this index span pretty much all industries and states. It's definitely a great place to start a career search.

For those of you, like me, however, who have an entrepreneurial spirit and are willing to take a gamble on yourself, my suggestion is to make your own job or create your own supplemental income streams. Find something you are passionate about and figure out how to make money doing just that. I spent so many years working for myself that I got spoiled, and frankly, I didn't want to go back to being an ordinary employee, working my ass off to pay for someone else's dream.

When I first started working in my own business, I had no clue what I was doing, and we didn't make enough to pay us a salary, so Jayna and I still had to have other jobs. I worked full-time doing massage therapy for a major casino on the Las Vegas Strip and any day off or free time went into building and learning the new business. I found great people in the advertising and marketing profession to latch onto, ask questions of, and shadow. I didn't go to college for this career, so I was definitely a fish out of water, but being willing to give it my best shot, make mistakes, and learn from others, I eventually figured it out. Many times, I thought I would never be good enough to live up to the company's expectations, but by teaming up with the right people who were more than willing to take me under their wings, I grew into my profession. I learned marketing and advertising by living it every day in real-life situations, applying what I learned, and hopefully, recognizing my mistakes and not repeating them. And in the end, isn't that what everyone is trying to do in any given career, whether you have the degree or not?

What I'm trying to say is: Don't let anyone, including yourself, tell you that you can't do something. If you don't have the proper credentials, find your passion and seek out those who are already doing what you wish you were and badger the hell out of them. Within reason, of course, but don't take a few no's to heart. I've heard Patrick Snow say numerous times, "If you want what others have, you must do what others have done, and you will get what others have gotten." That may mean having to take a few shit jobs in the meantime to pay some bills or gain the necessary experience to move forward, but never settle for mediocrity or lose sight of the light at the end of the tunnel. Again, visualize yourself as a success, as if you have already achieved the end result, and then go get it. For those of us who are transgender, that is exactly what we have done. We had a vision of the person we were meant to be, could visualize ourselves as that person, and made it happen.

Every job I've ever had has taught me something, whether positive or negative, but I've taken those lessons with me and they have helped to shape my future career. Knowing what I want, as well as what I won't accept, is priceless. I came to most of these realizations when I sat down and made a list of the things I liked to do, no matter how far-fetched. I had this big long list, and the top few things on it were: talk to people, have my own schedule, sleep in, work from home, and spend time with my dogs. It may sound funny, but those things are truly important to me. I can't think of many careers that check all those boxes, especially sleeping in, unless you're working a graveyard shift. But I kept looking at that list and tried to come up with ideas for how I could make that happen. I figured out a way to combine all those things into a career, one that I was willing to go after full force. My list had a wide range of topics; some had nothing to do with a career and wouldn't apply, but I still wrote everything down that I liked or wished I could do.

Make your own list and don't let "should" get in the way; list everything you can think of, no matter how out there it might seem. Maybe on your list, you love playing video games or are great with computers. Think of ways to do those things full time. I know people who design video games for a living or test them out and give reviews. It seems like new phone apps come out all the time and people pay to have them. Maybe you have an idea for an app that everyone will want or need; who knows? If you love to write, why not write a book? Trust me; if I can do it, so can you. And I know for a fact that there are millions of transgender men and women around the world who have had remarkable journeys, but their stories are not getting out there. We are under-represented. If you love to write, but a book isn't for you, become an editor or ghostwriter for someone else, or start up a tutoring business. Anyone can be an entrepreneur.

When I found out what my true passion was, I got to the point where I was willing to jump into the deep end of a waterless pool and have enough faith that there would be water when I landed.

Even though I was scared to share my story with the world, I continued to write. Many times during my early transition, I told myself that I just wanted to blend into society, and I was thankful that there were other transgender people who had the courage to speak up for people like me. I didn't think I would ever be ready to live out loud, but times changed, and so did I. Now that my book is finished, I will pound the pavement and speak to as many groups and organizations as will listen and want to know more about what being transgender is. And according to my list, hopefully none of the speaking engagements will start before 10 a.m. so I can sleep in!

I'm ready to take this gamble on myself until I've exhausted all possibilities, and not until then will I even consider a different path. Deep down, everyone has that kind of resolve, but we rarely tap into it because of fear and internal or external voices claiming otherwise. If any of you have a list but think you can't manifest a career you love, I invite you to contact me and together we will brainstorm outside the box. Turn your interests and passions into a money-making reality. Everyone has interests, talents, and hobbies that can be combined into a career with a little imagination. Just picture it—a career that you love and where being transgender doesn't matter because you are the boss. You won't have to live in fear of losing your job, nor will you be passed over for a promotion.

I have learned over the years in business and in life that if I perceive any obstacles, I can figure out a way to overcome them. If I can change genders, mid-life, I know I can create not only a successful career, but also a healthy and happy life for myself. And so can anyone else.

YOU ARE NOT ALONE

A FINAL NOTE

"Be strong enough to stand alone, smart enough to know when you need help, and brave enough to ask for it."

— Author Unknown

Being transgender can often be extremely lonely, scary, and confusing. Most of us hide who we truly are from the world, keeping it a deep dark secret that eats away at our souls until we either embrace our uniqueness and "come out," bury ourselves deeper, or, for many, commit suicide.

According to the Trevor Project website (www.thetrevorproject.org), "Nearly half of young transgender people have seriously thought about taking their lives, and one quarter report having made a suicide attempt." Many online articles echo that the suicide rate among transgender people, young or old, is alarmingly high. I could've easily been a statistic as well. It was by the grace of God and the fact that I finally reached out for help that I am still here.

For me, asking for help felt like a weakness, like I wasn't able to do something myself, but nothing could be further from the truth. Trying to go through life without help and support from others, whether you're trans or not, is difficult and isolating. I had convinced myself that no one would want to help me even if I asked, or that I would be a burden, so I said nothing. The truth is, we all like to help other people, really be there for them, and make a difference, but I robbed those around me from that opportunity. I kept pushing my friends further away, but like all true, good friends, they hung back at a safe distance, but never disappeared. When I finally opened up and said out loud that I needed them, my friends were more than willing to step up. It's as if they had been watching and waiting, knowing that day would come.

So why am I saying not to isolate yourself and hide who you truly are, even though that's exactly what I did, as I've detailed throughout this book? That's easy: Do as I say, not as I do! If that logic is good enough for parents, then it's good enough for me. Just as older generations like to bestow nuggets of wisdom to those younger in hopes of preventing the same painful mistakes they made, that's what I'm hoping to do for you as well. If just one person heeds that advice and doesn't have to know the pain associated with decades of loneliness, anxiety, and despair, then it's all worth it. I know that each and every one of us has our own journey to navigate, and yes, we do learn from our mistakes, but we don't have to make the same ones.

What's important for most people is to be accepted, loved, and supported. That is especially true for those who are transgender. It's not hard to find someone who rejects, ridicules, and judges others; just watch TV or nose around the Internet. If you happen to read the comment section of any story or video involving a transgender person, then you have seen how narrow-minded, rude, and cruel people can be, but know that there are so many amazing and supportive transgender allies out there to make up for the haters. And no one is ever truly alone. The trick is to concentrate your time and focus on those around you who have your back and love you just as you are. Now I'm totally blessed that that core group is my immediate family, but for so many, that isn't the case. I know plenty of transgender people who have been disowned or physically hurt by their families, just for being brave enough to live an authentic life. Unfortunately, that's a reality, so those of us who have a family safety net need to be mindful to reach out to those who need us. I can't speak about what it's like to be disowned, thrown out, or made to deny my true gender identity because that hasn't been my experience, and I would be lying if I said I could relate in any way. But even though that wasn't my journey, I can still be a lifeline for someone who is walking that path.

Going stealth or disappearing into male culture undetected is a goal for many trans guys; for a while, it was my goal too, but over time, I chose to take a different route because completely disappearing wasn't what I had hoped it to be. Because I didn't want anyone to know I was transgender, another trans guys who was struggling and needed help wouldn't be able to reach out to me because I couldn't be found.

What really brought this realization to light for me was when I moved back to Boulder the last time and a dear friend, who knew my past, mentioned that she had met a woman who had a transgender son, and he was very early in transition. It wasn't easy to be the parent watching all of these changes and not knowing what to say or do. Where was the manual? My friend asked whether it was okay to talk about my experience and me with this woman. I really appreciated that she asked me first, so I could choose whether or not to share a part of myself. She then wanted to know whether I would be willing to speak with her friend, so she could meet a trans guy who had gone through the same things that her son would be embarking on, and who had not only made it through transition, but was now happy and thriving as a man. She thought I could reassure this woman that her son would be just fine and become a well-adjusted, successful young man.

To be honest, my first gut reaction was, "Oh, shit!" I had blended in now, so I didn't want to be seen through the lens of my past, but that reaction only lasted a few minutes, and then I thought of my own parents and how I wished they had had someone to talk to. How great it would have been for my parents to be able to ask questions, to get a glimpse of what my future would be like, and to have some of their anxieties eased. It's easier to ask a stranger questions because there is less stress and tension and probably a more open dialogue. So I agreed to meet this woman, hoping it would ease her apprehension when she saw that I was just an average guy—a man who was successful, educated, and for the most part, had his shit together. That's what transgender looks like. It's not scary or freakish, and probably, not that unique.

When I met with this woman for coffee, she seemed a bit nervous, which was understandable, but she was also a bit relieved. I hope she saw this experience as being almost like meeting the future version of her new son, and that she realized she did not need to be afraid of the changes, but just to relax and enjoy the ride. She will have an opportunity to watch her child blossom into a happy and confident person whom he otherwise wouldn't be. I don't know of any parent who enjoys seeing his or her child miserable, even suicidal. Meeting with this woman was a wonderful experience for me as well because it was nice to talk freely about my experiences and share my transgendered journey. I talked about the ups and downs, and it was a great reminder to me that I'm truly okay and happy. I am finally content and at peace with myself. I am no longer searching. I wouldn't have changed anything in my life because all of it was necessary to get me to the man I am today. I think this brief get-together was helpful to her as well; at least, she said it was, and I'm learning to trust what people say. Eventually, I met her son and we have developed a nice friendship. Being a mentor or "big brother" is a win-win for both involved. He will know that he's not alone; someone else has had the same crazy thoughts and has done the same stupid things.

As I share my stories, it helps me to process my own transition since I tried to rush through it. It's like I can almost go back and enjoy the journey through someone else's eyes. But by no means am I saying that all transgender people need to be mentors, sounding boards, or even tell their stories at all. That is such a personal decision that does not have a wrong answer. It isn't for everyone, that's for sure, but if given the opportunity to help someone else struggling through the same things, your being visible can change someone else's life. The opportunity may never arise and you may never have to give this a second thought, but the way technology is advancing, making the world a much smaller place, odds are you may come across someone at some time who may need help, whether he or she asks for it or not. Many transgender people feel invisible and misunderstood, so having just one person acknowledge who you really are, letting you know that you are not alone, is priceless.

I'm thankful that I transitioned now, in a time that has more knowledge and support for transgender people than ever before. Even though we still have a long way to go, progress is being made. We live in an age where the term transgender is talked about and part of our mainstream language. Whether people agree with it or not, they at least recognize the term transgender and loosely know what it means. When I was growing up in the '70s and '80s, I had never heard the term, nor had I met anyone who was transgender. It just wasn't talked about, which made me feel like I was crazy and the only one in the world struggling to fit in. All I knew was that I was miserable because nothing made sense. Every ounce of myself felt and thought like a boy, but my body was doing something totally different. And because there was no dialogue about this, I had to live a painful and confused life trying to be the gender that matched my outward appearance.

All the time I was acting like a girl, I never felt like one, and I certainly never wanted that as my future. I sometimes wonder what my life would have been like if I had known just one other transgender person growing up or had even heard of such a thing. Would I have transitioned much earlier, saving myself from many years of depression? Who knows? But my hope in writing this book is that someone who reads it will feel less alone, less confused, and know that the necessary changes can be made to live the life he or she was meant to. I hope I have put into words the thoughts and fears others are experiencing, and hopefully, I can guide them in a positive direction to find the help and resources they need, to show that it does, in fact, get better. Or maybe by sharing my story out loud, I can take the pressure off another transgender person who doesn't want to share his or hers just yet, but has family, friends, or coworkers who want to know more. No one should ever feel obligated to share his or her personal struggles, but I made the choice to live out loud; it was a calling, something that I was compelled to do. I was ready, willing, and able, and if my book allows someone else who isn't ready to stay in his or her safe place, then I am happy to do it.

If I only help one person, then I have accomplished everything I set out to do by writing this book. Not only for those who are transgender, or questioning, but for their families and friends as well. Those of you who are supporting us in our journey also need support and guidance. I think of the people in my own support system and how my ups and downs affected them daily. They managed to deal with their own grief of losing the person I used to be, they learned to call me by my new name and use the correct pronouns, and they did all of that silently and by themselves. Sure, transitioning is difficult for any trans person, but it's easy to forget how difficult it is on those we love and care about. They are transitioning too. We've had our whole lives to wrestle with this situation, but those around us have to catch up on the fly. So if they can't or don't have open communication with their trans relative or friend, maybe this book will act as a surrogate in some way—a glimpse into what we go through and have struggled with our entire lives.

Many times throughout my life, I have thought I wouldn't make it or even hoped that I wouldn't, all because life was just too much of a struggle. And now that I have transitioned and am walking my truth, I still, at times, wonder, "Am I strong enough? Can I achieve what I set out to do?" When I fall prey to that negative way of thinking, that's when I ask for help. I have learned that I no longer have to go it alone and that I never did. When I opened up and let in those who truly wanted to help and support me, things always got better, but when I tried to go it alone, everything became larger than life and overwhelming. With just one person by my side, life is more manageable and enjoyable.

When I set out to write this book, I wrestled with a lot of internal self-sabotage and almost convinced myself that I couldn't do it; was I capable of putting words to paper or strong enough to tell my story? But again, I asked for help and have had it every step of the way. As Nelson Mandela said, "It always seems impossible until it's done." Through this process, I have had an opportunity to look back and reflect on my life and transition, which has opened my eyes to my faults, challenges, and self-imposed obstacles, all of which I create. It has also helped me to see my strengths, courage, and resilience. But most importantly, I have learned to look at myself in the mirror and not only like, but also love, what I see. I am more than okay; I am perfectly me.

RESOURCES

"Live the life you have imagined."
— Henry David Thoreau

SUPPORT/INFORMATION

American Civil Liberties Union (ACLU)
www.aclu.org

The Center – Denver
GLBT Community Center
www.glbtcolorado.org
(303) 733-7743

The Center – Las Vegas
GLBT Community Center
www.thecenterlv.org
(702) 733-9800

FTM Resource Guide
www.ftmguide.org

FTM Fitness World
www.ftmfitnessworld.com

FTM International
www.ftmi.org
(877) 267-1440

Gay & Lesbian Alliance Against Defamation (GLAAD)
www.glaad.org

Gender Identity Center of Colorado
www.gic-colorado.org

Gender Justice Nevada
Community Organization
www.gjnv.org

Human Rights Campaign (HRC)
www.hrc.org

It Gets Better Project
www.itgetsbetter.org

Laura's Playground
Transgender Support site
www.lauras-playground.com

National Center for Transgender Equality
www.transequality.org
(202) 903-0112

Parents, Families & Friends of Lesbians and Gays (PFLAG)
Family & Ally Organization
www.pflag.org
(202) 467-8180

Peecock Products
FTM prosthetics, STPs, Binders
www.peecockproducts.com

RESOURCES

Selective Service
www.sss.gov
(888) 655-1825

Matthew Shepard Foundation
www.matthewshepard.org

Social Security Administration
www.ssa.gov
(800) 772-1213

Suicide Prevention Lifeline
www.suicidepreventionlifeline.org
(800) 273-8255

The Trevor Project
Crisis Intervention & Suicide Prevention
www.thetrevorproject.org
(866) 488-7386

Transgender Law Center
www.transgenderlawcenter.org
(415) 865-0176

Transgender & Transsexual Road Map
Transition Guide
www.TSRoadmap.com

Transitional Male
Transmen Resources
www.thetransitionalmale.com

Transforming Family
Family Support
www.transformingfamily.org
(855) 543-7436

271

TransYouth Family Allies
Family & Transgender Youth Support
www.imatyfa.org
(888) 462-8932

Youth Resource
www.youthresource.org

HEALTHCARE

Sandi Daileda
Intuitive Healer
Super Healing Arts Studio
www.superhealingarts.com
(303) 499-1337

Nextera Healthcare
www.nexterahealthcare.com
(303) 501-2600

North Vista Medical Center
Dr. David Tusek, Dr. Clint Flanagan
www.northvistamedical.com
(303) 501-2600

SURGEONS

Brownstein Crane Surgery
www.brownsteincrane.com
Dr. Curtis Crane
(877) 255-2081

Marci Bowers, MD
www.marcibowers.com
(650) 570-2270

Miroslav Djordjevic, MD
www.genitalsurgerybelgrade.com

Charles Garramone, MD
www.drgarramone.com
(954) 752-7842

Christine McGinn, MD
Papillon Center
www.drchristinemcginn.com
(215) 693-1199

Toby R. Meltzer, MD
www.tmeltzer.com
(866) 876-6329

Transbucket
Healthcare/Surgery Guide
www.transbucket.com

TSsurgeryguide.com
Transgender Surgeon's Guide

SPEAKING/PUBLISHING

Patrick Snow
International Best-Selling Author
Professional Keynote Speaker
Publishing, Speaking & Book Marketing Coach
www.PatrickSnow.com
(206) 310-1200

Jeremy L. Wallace
Author
Professional Keynote Speaker
Jeremy@JeremyLWallace.com
www.JeremyLWallace.com
(303) 810-4071

ABOUT THE AUTHOR

JEREMY L. WALLACE is an author, professional keynote speaker, and entrepreneur. He has spent over twenty-five years of his life successfully going through a major transformation that has led him to find his inner truth. This experience has qualified him to become one of the leading speakers on transformative change.

Combining his expertise as an entrepreneurial business owner with life-challenging experiences, Jeremy speaks to corporations, organizations, and groups of any size about embracing change, becoming our true selves, and living up to our full potential.

Originally from Michigan, Jeremy graduated from the University of Colorado in 1994. He now resides in Las Vegas with his two dogs.

Visit Jeremy at www.JeremyLWallace.com

BOOK JEREMY L. WALLACE TO SPEAK AT YOUR NEXT EVENT

When it comes to choosing a speaker for your next event, you will find no one more capable of empowering and entertaining your audience than Jeremy. He has a way of captivating a crowd and uses humor to put people at ease when speaking on tough issues. Topics can be customized to meet the needs of school groups, organizations, or conferences. Sample topics include:

- Transgender education & equality
- Overcoming obstacles
- Finding your true self and passion
- Embracing change
- Living up to your full potential

Jeremy shares his stories of how he faced his fears and courageously overcame great obstacles to become the successful man he was destined to be. As he electrifies an audience of any size, in North America or abroad, Jeremy leaves his listeners believing they too can live up to their full potential.

www.JeremyLWallace.com
Jeremy@JeremyLWallace.com
(303) 810-4071